D0516897

FEAR OF FINANCE

FEAR OF FINANCE

THE
WOMEN'S
MONEY WORKBOOK
FOR ACHIEVING
FINANCIAL
SELF-CONFIDENCE

ANN B. DIAMOND

Illustrations by Lori Loebelsohn

HarperBusiness
A Division of HarperCollinsPublishers

FEAR OF FINANCE. Copyright © 1994 by Ann B. Diamond. All rights reserved.
Printed in the United States of America.
No part of this book may be used or reproduced in any manner whatsoever
without written permission except in the case of brief quotations
embodied in critical articles and reviews.
For information address
HarperCollins Publishers, Inc.,
10 East 53rd Street,
New York, NY 10022.

HarperCollins books may be purchased
for educational, business, or sales promotional use.
For information please write:
Special Markets Department,
HarperCollins Publishers, Inc.,
10 East 53rd Street,
New York, NY 10022.

FIRST EDITION

Designed by Ruth Kolbert

Library of Congress Cataloging-in-Publication Data

Diamond, Ann B., 1951–
Fear of finance: the women's money workbook for achieving
financial self-confidence / Ann B. Diamond. — 1st ed.
p.   cm.
ISBN 0-88730-625-X (pbk.)
1. Women—Finance, Personal.   I. Title.
HG179.D52   1994
332.024'042—dc20   93-21658

94 95 96 97 98 PS/RRD 10 9 8 7 6 5 4 3 2 1

For my parents, who prepared me well for the adventure of life.
And for Larry, who makes each day of my life an adventure.

CONTENTS

ACKNOWLEDGMENTS

What have I learned from writing this workbook? That no author writes a book alone; that friendship and support are critical; that keeping your eye on the goal applies to everything in life. Through the process I have developed a profound respect for writers—until you try writing, you can't appreciate the time, devotion, and pain that is a large part of the experience.

In fact, if I knew then what I know now, I'm certain I would have been totally intimidated from tackling this project, which was sparked by Ed Burlingame's interest in my financial seminars for women. Both Ed and Christa Weil nursed me through the initial stages with enormous kindness and skill and I am grateful for their faith in the concept of this book. My appreciation extends to my editor, Stephanie Gunning, whose inspired suggestions and contagious enthusiasm guided me through the most desperate moments. I thank my copy editor, Shelly Perron, and my production editor, Trent Duffy, for their meticulous reshaping of my work into a user-friendly workbook.

First, thanks to Melvin R. Seiden, for truly living up to the definition of mentor. I want to acknowledge my financial planning colleagues who provide assistance and encouragement: Connie Chen, Suzette Loh, and most expecially Barbara Levy, who offered her support every step of the way.

Special thanks to the many professionals who commented or offered recommendations on various parts of the manuscript: David Politziner, Linda Hamilton, Leslie Anker, Henry Alter, Margaret Scott, Theo

Fuchs, Judy Grossman, Melinda Lloyd, and Florence Fearrington. Also thanks to my investment group—Joan, Mary, Melinda, Pat, Janet, Janine, Florence, and Nan—for listening to my problems, offering solutions, and generally being a sounding board during all phases of this project.

I owe Bob Ortaldo much gratitude for allowing the use of his debt reduction technique in the credit section. I also want to acknowledge a Federal Reserve publication, *Consumer Handbook to Credit Protection Laws*. Much of the information in the credit chapter came from this excellent booklet.

I am grateful that my life and career have been shaped by my spiritual awareness; my parents; my husband, Larry; my stepdaughter, Lori; my brother, Don, and his family, and my dear friends.

And finally, thanks to Citibank MasterCard and Visa for giving me the privilege of being the spokesperson for Money Matters for Women. This has allowed me to meet women around the country, who have shared their experiences and questions with me. These women were the inspiration for this book.

INTRODUCTION

———————

Why did you buy this book? You want something, right? What is it? To be able to buy whatever you want . . . to be able to retire . . . to afford an education for your children . . . to be free from debt.

How badly do you want it? Is it just some vague feeling that comes and goes, or do you think about it all the time? Are you anxious because you know you should be doing something about it but aren't sure what?

Give yourself a pat on the back. You've taken the first step. You are about to take part in a seminar that I have been leading for more than six years. It's designed to get you organized, to help you formulate your goals, and to assist in the process of funding those goals. This workbook is unique because you will not be taking this course alone. You will be participating with five other women who, as you will learn, all have different reasons for being here. You may find you have a lot in common with one or maybe more than one of the women. Following their progress will make coming up with your own plan more interesting and, I hope, more fun.

The *only* prerequisite you need for this class is desire. You must want your money dream so much that you can touch it, feel it, and even see it. Visualizing your dream every day is helpful. Before you go to sleep, while semiconscious take yourself through the steps that will make it real. What you will be doing is conditioning your mind not only to accept your idea, but also to start making it happen.

We will speak a lot about motivation because it is the key to getting what you want. I can show you how to go through the steps, but without discipline and desire, you won't accomplish your goal. If this book winds up under a pile of other projects that you meant to do, you will have short-circuited a real opportunity to finally "get it together." Don't waste this moment.

Women tell me that one of the reasons they don't get their finances in order is because it is an overwhelming job. It touches every aspect of their lives, so knowing where to begin is hard. But something I learned in a time management course many years ago can help: When a job is too big, the way to get it done is to break it down into a number of smaller jobs. That is what we are going to do. Each chapter tackles one aspect of your financial management. Take your time, but *keep going*. Even if it takes you months, remember the benefits last the rest of your life!

Being a financial counselor, I believe people should get professional help, but I also believe that ultimately responsibility rests with you. This book will help you either develop your own plan or organize your thoughts so that you can make better use of a planner's services. Whichever way you go, always remember that *you* are the person who is making the decisions. It's your money and your life, and no one knows better than you what your priorities are.

I have always been inspired by the generous spirit of women and their desire to assist others in improving the quality of their lives. We can learn so much from one another. I hope that in joining our seminar you will share in the discovery that we each have the capacity to create a happier, more fulfilled existence for ourselves.

IN THE BEGINNING

ANN: Welcome. It's always such a pleasure to meet women who are motivated to take this course and spend the next few weeks together learning how to handle personal finances. When I came in you were all introducing yourselves—a good place to start. One of the joys of this seminar is getting to know one another. I promise, even the shyest among you will soon be speaking up about your money situation. But since so many people think money is a very personal topic, the more we know about one another, the easier it will be for us to share our experiences.

It might be helpful for you to know why I teach this seminar, how it came to exist, and what I hope you will accomplish. When I was a portfolio manager with a private investment-banking firm, I received requests from many of my friends for help with their financial management. These women all had good jobs and were well educated, but none of them seemed to have any idea what to do with the money once they earned it. It occurred to me that they were not alone. So I asked them all to attend a group of meetings in my home where they explained to me what they needed to learn, and together we created a seminar for women that provided many of the answers to their questions. Over the course of the next six years, I led seminars throughout the country and discovered that most women have the same basic concerns. They all feel their level of education is inadequate; they want to learn; they are distrustful of professionals; and they have a fear of making mistakes and losing money.

My motivation for leading this seminar is threefold: First, together we can open up the dialogue and dispel the fear that this is an "unfeminine" topic; second, we can take the mystique out of the subject and realize that it can be mastered and isn't as complicated as you imagine; and third, we can participate in the most wonderful feeling there is—knowing we are responsible and in control of our own destiny.

I would love each of you to share with us why you are here and what you hope to gain from this experience. Who wants to start?

CAROL: I'll start. I'm here because I got myself into a mess and I don't really know how to get out. I'm in my late forties. Three years ago I divorced my husband of 20 years. I have two girls; Christy is 12 and Judy is 14 and we are very close. The divorce has been difficult for both of them, and I have worked hard at keeping the relationship with my husband civil for their sake. But it isn't easy. I'm very resentful about the financial arrangement that was made, and I think that because my ex-husband is a lawyer and more financially savvy than myself, he somewhat took advantage of me. That may not be so, but it's how I feel.

I worked until I became pregnant with Judy, and then Jack and I decided that I would stay home to raise our family. I loved it and am very happy I had that time with my girls. The only thing I didn't like was that every month Jack would give me a certain amount of money for the family bills, and I would be in charge of the budget. When there were big expenses, like when we needed a new washing machine or when Judy needed braces for her teeth, I would have to ask him for more money, and I always felt nervous about it, even if it wasn't for a personal item. It was as if I had "wasted" the money I had been given and had to go back to "daddy" for more. I hated that.

Anyway, the divorce settlement granted me child support until the girls are over 18, and then Jack and I are equally responsible for their college education. The court ruled that I was to get alimony for five years to give me time to find a job and acclimate myself to a new life-style. But I haven't worked in over 15 years! I feel paralyzed. I need training and counseling, which I am currently looking into. I know that I *have* to get my act together and find employment. I am taking this course because I know I'm not going to make the kind of money I'm used to living on, and I need to learn how to manage the money better. In two years, I'll be without alimony, and even with it, my outgo is more than my income. I *refuse* to go begging to Jack for more money—I will not confirm his opinion that I am incompetent and wasteful. I am ready to take responsibility for my life and for my children.

ANN: Carol, you have already taken that first important step. You've realized on your own that the time is right to begin, and you have a real reason to stay motivated. As we begin the process, you'll see how significant desire is in getting the job done.

Who would like to speak next?

STACY

STACY: I guess I will. To tell you the truth, it was my parents' idea, and I'm not 100 percent sure why I'm here. I just graduated from college in May, and I have an internship at a publishing firm.

ANN: A paid internship?

STACY: I get paid, but not very much. I mean, I don't make enough to have my own apartment, so I'm living with my parents. When I finish with my training, I hope I'll be offered a real job and I'll make more. Right now, my parents are charging me rent and I pay my phone bill, but they take care of everything else. I want to save money now while my expenses are low so I can afford to get an apartment with a friend in about a year.

Actually, I feel I'm in a transition right now. Maybe it would have been better to take this class when I am a little more settled and begin my "real life."

ANN: Stacy, women of all ages think they are "in a transition" right now. Quite honestly, all of life is a transition. If you wait for your "real life" to begin, you may be approaching retirement before it dawns on you that you wasted many precious years. If your life isn't what you want it to be, then get busy and change it. But don't wait to take control of your finances. If you are single, it is much easier to start than if you are married, because you have only yourself to consult. You plan for *your* needs. Then, if you get married or have children, you will need to adjust the plan only to fit your new circumstances.

So let's try it again . . . Why are you here?

STACY: OK. I'm here because my dad says I don't know the value of money. How could I? He certainly didn't teach that to me, and I never took any personal finance classes in school either. I think he's still upset from the time I charged my trip during spring break on my credit card and then couldn't pay it back. He had to bail me out. One of my graduation presents was this course. At first I thought it was a punishment, but now that I'm here, I'm sort of looking forward to it. I want to learn how to be self-sufficient.

TERRY: I'm one of those people who was always taught that it was unfeminine to handle money. When I got married and my husband took over where my parents left off, I felt safe and protected. But last year my sister's husband died and I see what she is going through now. She has no idea where any of the papers are or even who her accountant is. I know a little more than she does, but certainly not enough to feel secure about my family's future. In fact, I have always had a math block; I guess that goes back to my upbringing. I was good in English and history but never really got the hang of math and science.

ANN: Let me interrupt you for a minute, Terry, because you have hit on something that a lot of women tell me, and maybe I can ease your mind. When you think of math, I'll bet you're recalling your study of algebra, geometry, calculus. You know, even the people who were good at these subjects in school don't remember too much about them now unless they use this kind of math in their work. We're not going to need any of that. All we use is simple arithmetic—adding, subtracting, multiplying, and dividing.

TERRY: I'm not too good at that either.

ANN: Not to worry. That's why calculators were born. We are concerned with concepts and understanding how to organize ourselves. Believe me, the math is the least of our problems.

Terry, I'm sorry I had to interrupt you. Please go on.

TERRY: I have three children; Mary is seven, William is five, and Jo is just two. My husband, Mike, is the police chief of our town. My life is so busy, between coordinating my children's schedules and the social obligations of Mike's job. I feel enormous anxiety because I want to protect my family, but I don't know where to start, and every time I make an attempt, the job seems so overwhelming that I just give up. My husband thinks that since my brother-in-law's death, I am developing a phobia. He heard about this seminar at work from an officer whose wife took it. It helped her enormously—I hope it will do the same for me.

ANN: It's interesting that most people become involved in the seminar when something happens in their life that makes them feel insecure about their future. Like you, Terry, someone close to them dies, or there is an accident, or they get divorced. I wish women wouldn't wait for a traumatic event to force them into action. Planning is easier when you have a clear head. On the other hand, whatever brings you to the realization that it is time to act brings you one step closer to independence, and it puts you way ahead of the people who just go back to bed and pull the covers over their head and hope the worry will disappear.

JANE: That sounds like a perfect introduction for me. I'm 62 years old and almost three years ago my husband died. Ann, what you said about trying to deal with the finances during a traumatic event is absolutely true. I couldn't concentrate on anything! It was like I was in a fog, observing the events of my life without any ability to make decisions. So many people offered me advice, it just made me more confused. I know they had my best interest at heart, but how could *they* have any idea what I was going to do; *I* had no idea what I was going to do.

So, I took the insurance money and any other cash that wasn't invested, and I stuck it in the bank. It's been sitting there for all this time because I figured it was safe there until I felt confident enough to make investment decisions. It's taken me up until now to feel like the fog is lifting. I'm facing the fact that the finances are now my total responsibility. You know, when you are married for almost 40 years, it takes some time to deal with the reality of being alone.

I want to get on with my life, and I have some very big decisions to make. Do I want to sell my house, do I want to retire from my job, can I *afford* to retire from my job? If I do retire, do I want to move to a warmer climate? I would miss my friends and grandchildren terribly, but the children are getting older, they have their own lives and don't have that much time to spend with me.

I guess it's obvious, but coming out of the fog can be very confusing. What I'm excited about with this seminar is that you all seem so honest and supportive. I need to talk this out with some people who can be more objective than my children or my friends. They all have their own agendas for me.

ANN: You need to find *your* own agenda, Jane. And we're here to help you. Susan, we still haven't heard from you.

SUSAN: I am like the women you described when you talked about how you started the seminar in the first place. I have been working in advertising for over 20 years. People think I have a very glamorous existence: I live in a nice apartment, I travel to Europe twice a year, I buy good clothes, sometimes even at retail! I rent a beach house every summer.

STACY: Sounds great to me.

SUSAN: I can't complain about my life-style. I grew up seeing how the traditional system did not work for my mother. My parents were divorced when I was eight years old, and my mother worked two low-paying jobs. I vowed I would *never* let that happen to me, and so I worked my way through school and got a job in advertising because I heard you could make a lot of money. I became obsessed with my job to the exclusion of everything else. And I succeeded. I am vice president of my firm, in charge of new business. But even though I make a lot of money, I spend more than I make, which is hard for me to understand. But it seems to be a fact, since I can't really figure out where it goes. It's ridiculous. I work with budgets all day long on the job, but when it comes to my own, I'm a wreck.

My most important goal always was to have a career. Even so, I somehow always assumed I would get married. Now that I'm forty-something, it has occurred to me that I might remain single forever. If I don't start to plan for the future, I may never be able to stop working. Or even worse, if I lose my job, I have no investments and no emergency fund. I know no knight in shining armor is going to rescue me. I have to save myself. Lately, I have been having this recurring nightmare that I'm a bag lady, homeless and alone. I have always been a take-charge kind of person. I took this dream as a signal that I needed help. Although I probably could also use a therapist, I thought coming to this seminar would be an immediate step in the right direction.

ANN: One of the fascinating points many of you brought up bears discussion. All of us form our opinions about money from what we learned and observed in our homes. It is obviously very subjective and explains why there are so many misconceptions and emotional issues surrounding the topic.

While we'll discuss these feelings together, our main goal isn't pinning down how we got our money problems, but instead it's *solving* them. We want to figure out where our finances are right now and then learn basic facts about money and investing that we were never taught at home or in school, and apply them to a step-by-step approach of financial management. We'll all have more knowledge of how we can make money fulfill our dreams. I hope we'll also learn how our perceptions of what we can do influence our ability to accomplish our goals. We'll get started on that in our next lesson.

GOAL SETTING

PART I

ANN: When I ask people what their financial goals are, the answer I hear most often is "I want to be rich!" Although this is honest and deeply felt, it's not specific enough. Why do you want to be rich? Do you want to retire and live in Tahiti for the rest of your life? Do you want to be a philanthropist and help people in need? Until you define what you are trying to accomplish, the exercises in this course will have no purpose.

"Why" you ask? Because the key to financial security and happiness is directing our attention toward specific goals. Many of us spend our lives going from emergency to emergency without ever accumulating any wealth. We need to motivate ourselves to "invest in" our dreams. The only way to do this is to write down what we want. When you see your goals in print, they become more real. With our first worksheet you will clearly define your short-term (one year or less), medium-term (two to five years) and long-term (more than five years) goals.

We'll begin with the Goals Worksheet. Here you will write down whatever goals/dreams come to mind, placing them under the short-, medium-, or long-term heading. But before filling in anything, let's discuss our goals a bit.

STACY: I want to build a whole new wardrobe for work. I wish I could move out of my parents' house and live on my own, but it costs so much, and I would need to buy a car. There are so many things I would like to buy: a CD player, a new TV, an exercise bike. I might want to go back to school for an advanced degree some time in the future. Oh, and I almost forgot. I owe my parents money for my last trip, which I want to pay off, and I'd love to plan my next vacation.

Goals Worksheet *I*

	STACY	TERRY	SUSAN	CAROL	JANE	YOU
SHORT-TERM (1 yr.)	Wardrobe Travel CD player TV Exercise bike Pay loan from parents	Fix sink Paint house	Tax planning Life insurance	Get job Pay credit card debt	Health insurance Travel	
MEDIUM-TERM (2–5 yrs.)	Move Buy car Advanced degree	Move Part-time job College fund Furniture	Beach house Investment portfolio	Keep home College fund	Move Retire Long-term-care insurance	
LONG-TERM (5+ yrs.)	——	Own business	Retirement fund	Retirement fund	——	

TERRY: My kitchen sink has been leaking for a month. The house needs painting and I am still using furniture from my relatives. We have been renting a small two-bedroom house since we were married. Now with three children, we really need more space. I want my children to go to college, and I want to be able to work part-time—maybe have my own business in my home.

SUSAN: I need to do something about all the taxes I pay. I do own a cooperative apartment, but I don't have much in the way of investments. I would love to own a beach house instead of renting each summer. And I have enormous anxiety about my retirement. I don't have any life insurance, and this worries me too.

CAROL: When my alimony ends in two years, I will need to work. I receive child support, but it is minimal and will end when the girls are 18 years old. I want to keep my home until my children go off to school. My ex-husband has to share the responsibility for their college education, but at the rate I'm going, I will *never* be able to afford half of the cost. I need to feel secure about what will happen to me and ensure my daughters' futures. I also *must* find a way to pay off all the credit card debt I have accumulated.

JANE: I want to retire and be able to travel and perhaps move to a warmer climate. I want to make sure I have enough money to live comfortably. I am concerned about my health and if I'm adequately covered in case I become very ill. My children are very supportive, but they have their children to take care of. I don't want to be dependent on them.

ANN: These are all positive, achievable goals, but there's one more nobody mentioned. A short-term goal I would like you all to have is establishing an emergency fund. This would cover six months of fixed expenses (rent, utilities, etc.—items you must pay *every* month without fail). You relieve a lot of anxiety when you have money available in case of illness or job loss. You'll have a clearer idea of how much of an emergency fund you should have on hand when we work on our Cash Flow Worksheet later on.

TERRY: Wait a minute. "Cash flow," "emergency fund," "fixed expenses." All this terminology scares me. Do we have to learn another language to handle our finances?

ANN: Every field has its own language. But you mastered the words necessary to cook your favorite recipe, right? Or learned the terminology to play tennis or golf or any other sport. For some reason, the language of finance can seem more intimidating, but I promise that you'll begin to feel comfortable with the financial lingo as you proceed through this course. Besides, I'll be defining the most important terms as we go along.

Goals Worksheet II

	STACY	TERRY	SUSAN	CAROL	JANE	YOU
SHORT-TERM (1 yr.)	Emergency fund Wardrobe Travel ~~CD player~~ ~~TV~~ ~~Exercise bike~~ Pay loan from parents	Emergency fund Fix sink Paint house Car Vacation Life insurance	Emergency fund Tax planning ~~Life insurance~~ Disability insurance	Emergency fund Get job Pay credit card debt Job-skill counseling Wardrobe Life insurance	Emergency fund Health insurance Travel	Emergency fund
MEDIUM-TERM (2–5 yrs.)	Move Buy car Advanced degree	Move Part-time job College fund Furniture	Beach house Investment portfolio Volunteer Collect furniture	Keep home College fund	Move Retire Long-term-care insurance	
LONG-TERM (5+ yrs.)	Retirement fund	Own business	Retirement fund Spend more time as volunteer	Retirement fund	Part-time job/business Leave money for grandchildren	

CAROL: What do we do once we have filled in our goals?

ANN: Sleep on these first thoughts. We have planted a seed, and you will be dreaming about what you really want. In a few days, revisit the Goals I Worksheet and make revisions. Take out any items that seem less important and add items you hadn't thought of before. When you return for the next session, we will discuss your revised versions.

Reader, now is the time to grab a pencil and fill in *your* goals on the Goals I Worksheet. After a day or so, take another look and revise as necessary, on Goals II, opposite.

LESSON 3

▆▆ ▆▆ ▆ ▆ ▆▆ ▆▆ ▆ ▆▆▆▆ ▆▆ ▆▆ ▆▆▆ ▆▆ ▆▆ ▆▆ ▆ ▆▆ ▆▆▆ ▆▆▆▆▆▆▆▆▆

GOAL SETTING

PART II

▆▆▆▆ ▆▆ ▆

ANN: Did everyone make changes to her original list?

STACY: I couldn't think of any long-term goals when I first did this exercise. It's hard for me to think beyond five years! But hearing everyone else's thoughts makes me feel nervous about my retirement. I think I should add that to my list. I really don't need the CD player or the new TV. And since I go to the health club regularly, I don't need an exercise bike at home.

TERRY: I realized I hadn't taken my husband into consideration when I formulated my list. He really needs a new car—I'm worried every time he goes out in our old one. It also would be very nice for us to have a short vacation without the children. Another concern I have is how my husband would cope if I should die. He would definitely need help with the children, but how could he afford hiring someone? I think I should have a life insurance policy that would provide the money.

ANN: That makes a lot of sense, Terry. Many homemakers don't realize how valuable their contribution is in terms of running the home and taking care of the children. But think about what it would cost to hire someone to replace you. When determining how much life insurance both partners need, you should figure out what amount each person brings to the family in wages or services. Then purchase a policy that will enable your partner to invest the principal and use the income to make up for the shortfall.

SUSAN: Speaking of insurance, I found out by talking to my sister's insurance agent that I don't really need life insurance, since I have no children or other dependents to protect. The insurance I need is disability, which protects my income in case I become ill and can't work.

Somehow, when I thought about my goals, it never occurred to me that I should include some dreams I have always had. I would love to collect fine country furniture. Also, I have never had time to help others, and I would like to volunteer to aid the literacy campaign with a thought to becoming more active in it once I retire or semi-retire.

CAROL: In order to get into the work force again, I'm going to need job-skill counseling. Also, I'll need new clothes, which I hadn't thought about until Stacy mentioned it. Susan may not need life insurance, but I certainly do. I have none; what would happen to my girls if I died?

JANE: It might be nice to have a part-time job, or start a small business once I retire. I would also like to leave some money for my grandchildren's education.

ANN: Now that we have a firm idea of our goals, we're ready for the next worksheet, entitled Goals III. Here we're going to quantify each of our goals, which means estimating the cost of each item. For example, if you're planning a vacation, are you going away for a long weekend, or are you taking a three-week tour of Europe? Obviously, the amount of money you'll be spending will vary significantly.

There may be some goals that you don't know enough about to be able to put a dollar figure on. This is OK—you can put a question mark next to it, and after investigating, fill it in. For example, let's take your emergency fund. Until you work on your cash flow, which we'll do in lesson 7, you will not know how much money is required to cover your fixed expenses for six months. Either leave the amount blank or estimate what you think it is. We will revise it later.

For most women retirement will be one of their long-term goals. You cannot at this point know how much money you'll need to retire. (We'll work on this later in the book, too.) You'll need to set aside an amount of money per year in order to create a retirement fund. The younger you are, the less you'll need to put away each year, because time and compounding over a long period of time make this task much easier. It is advisable to take advantage of your company plans—401(k), thrift, etc.—to the maximum possible, because there are tax benefits and often matching contributions from your firms.

With this in mind, let's fill in the sheet entitled Goals Worksheet III. Reader, fill yours in along with us.

*　　*　　*

Goals Worksheet III

	STACY	TERRY	SUSAN	CAROL	JANE	YOU
SHORT-TERM (1 yr.)	Emergency fund ? Wardrobe $1,500 Travel $1,000 Pay loan from parents $1,300	Emergency fund ? Fix sink $150–200 Paint house $1,000–1,500 Car $10,000–12,000 Vacation $1,000 Life Insurance $200–500/year	Emergency fund ? Tax planning Disability insurance $1,000–2,000?	Emergency fund ? Get job Job-skill counseling $500? Pay credit card debt $11,000 Wardrobe $2,000 Life insurance $250–300/year	Emergency fund ? Health insurance $1,000–1,500/year Travel $2,500	Emergency fund ?
MEDIUM-TERM (2–5 yrs.)	Move $3,500 Buy used car $5,000 Advanced degree ?	Move—down payment and moving $40,000 Part-time job College fund $2,000/child/year Furniture $5,000	Beach house $200,000 Investment portfolio $10,000/year Volunteer Collect furniture $2,500/year	Keep home $10,000/year College fund $3,000/child/year	Move $10,000 Retire ? Long-term-care insurance $1,000–2,000/year?	
LONG-TERM (5+ yrs.)	Retirement fund $1,000/year	Own business $15,000 (inventory)	Retirement fund $7,500–9,000/year Spend more time as volunteer	Retirement fund $2,000/year	Part-time job/business Leave money for grandchildren $10,000/child	

Goals Worksheet IV

	STACY	TERRY	SUSAN	CAROL	JANE	YOU
SHORT-TERM (1 yr.)	1. Emergency fund ? 2. Wardrobe $1,500 4. Travel $1,000 3. Pay loan from parents $1,300	1. Emergency fund ? 3. Fix sink $150–200 5. Paint house $1,000–1,500 4. Car $10,000–12,000 6. Vacation $1,000 2. Life insurance $200–250	2. Emergency fund ? 3. Tax planning 1. Disability insurance $1,000–2,000?	2. Emergency fund ? 5. Get job 4. Job-skill counseling $500? 1. Pay credit card debt $11,000 6. Wardrobe $2,000 3. Life insurance $250–300	1. Emergency fund ? 2. Health insurance $1,000–1,500 3. Travel $2,500	Emergency fund ?
MEDIUM-TERM (2–5 yrs.)	2. Move $3,500 1. Buy used car $5,000 3. Advanced degree?	1. Move $40,000 3. Part-time job 2. College fund $2,000/child/year 4. Furniture $5,000	1. Beach house $200,000 2. Investment portfolio $10,000 4. Volunteer 3. Collect furniture $2,500/year	1. Keep home $10,000/year 2. College fund $3,000/child/year	2. Move $10,000 1. Retire ? 3. Long-term-care insurance $1,000–2,000/year	
LONG-TERM (5+ yrs.)	1. Retirement fund $1,000/year	1. Own business $15,000 (inventory)	1. Retirement fund $7,500–9,000/year 2. Spend more time as volunteer	1. Retirement fund $2,000/year	2. Part-time job/business 1. Leave money for grandchildren $10,000/child	

All set? In the next worksheet, Goals IV, we will set our priorities. If we could accomplish only *one* or *two* goals over the next few years, what would they be? This will allow you to focus on the items that are important to you and motivate you to create a system to provide the money for these items. Number each goal in the short-term, medium-term, and long-term categories from Goals III, and put them in the proper order. Reader, look at how the others have prioritized and then number your own goals. *Do not rush through this step.* Take your time, consider and reconsider, because knowing what's most important will help everything else fall into place.

Congratulations! You have just completed the most difficult step in the entire financial planning process—figuring out what you want to accomplish. You are on the way to fulfilling your goals. There are three other crucial ingredients to making it happen:

1. *Discipline.* You must be religious about allocating money toward your goals from *every* paycheck, not just when you have extra (which will be seldom, if ever).

Aim to dedicate 10 percent of your gross income toward financing your objectives. In other words, if you earn $20,000 per year, $2,000 is the magic number to save. If that is not possible right now, begin with 3 percent of your income. Then every six months or when you get a raise or bonus, increase the amount by 1 percent. For example, if your income is $20,000, begin with 3 percent of $20,000 or $600 per year. Saving $600 per year is $50 per month or $25 per paycheck (if you are paid twice a month). Now, let's say you get a raise to $21,000. Increase your funding to $35 per paycheck, which would yield you $840 per year (4 per-

INTEREST GROWTH CHART
$2,000 invested per year, at 10% annual interest

NUMBER OF YEARS CONTRIBUTED	TOTAL CONTRIBUTION	AMOUNT PRODUCED	
		IF PAYING TAX ON EARNINGS (28%)	IN A TAX-DEFERRED ACCOUNT
5	$ 10,000	$ 12,379	$ 13,431
10	20,000	29,904	35,062
15	30,000	54,714	69,899
20	40,000	89,838	126,005
25	50,000	139,563	216,364
30	60,000	209,960	361,887
35	70,000	309,621	596,254

cent of $21,000). Within a few years, you will be investing 10 percent of your income toward your future goals, and because you did it gradually and systematically, it will not be a strain. And, most important, between your contributions and the miracle of compounding, you will be accumulating the money necessary to make your dreams come true. (If you want to see how much $2,000, invested every year and earning 10 percent interest, will grow into, see the table on p. 16.)

This brings me to the second ingredient:

2. *Time.* The longer you have, the easier it will be to accumulate the money necessary.

The third ingredient in achieving financial fitness is:

3. *Motivation.* The reason we set our goals first is because it is easier to save money for something specific than for an unidentified "ideal." You need to want your goals so intensely that only a *true* emergency could keep you from diverting the amount from your funding account.

TERRY: I must say, I was very nervous when I first walked into this seminar. I thought I would be the dumbest one, and that I wouldn't even understand what anyone was talking about. I'm so relieved to find that the anxiety I felt is gone! For the first time, I feel confident that I can really do this.

CAROL: Ha! You thought *you* would be the dumbest. That's a laugh. During my divorce proceedings, I realized how little I really knew about this subject. Since then, I have been in hiding—literally. . . . Anytime a decision needed to be made, I would find another closet to clean. I'm finally beginning to feel that I'll be able to cope with taking care of my girls on my own.

STACY: How could the two of you know less than I know? I haven't even begun working at a real job yet. Somebody has always taken care of me. I have to say, when my parents gave me this seminar as a gift I wasn't too thrilled, but now I see how useful it will be. I'm lucky to learn all this *before* I make a lot of mistakes.

ANN: Stacy, basically I like what I hear from you, but let's not worry too much about making mistakes. Sometimes, all of us try strategies that need changing or modification. We don't want to paralyze ourselves into making no decision just because we don't want to make an error. There are times when taking a risk is appropriate. We'll talk more about that later on, when we discuss investing in lesson 12. I also want to address your concerns about appearing "dumb." No one ever taught you this material, so how could you be expected to know it? I am proud of you for taking the initiative to learn it on your own *now.*

JANE: I knew before I began this seminar that my main goal was to be able to retire. Somehow writing it down, and getting more specific about the details of when and how, has made me want to forge ahead. How do we get started?

ANN: I'm glad you are excited to begin. Now that we've established what we really want to accomplish and believe in its importance so strongly that we are willing to make it a priority, we can proceed to the next lessons in this seminar. Just to preview, there will be worksheets that will help you figure out where your money situation stands today (this is called a Net Worth Statement). You'll discover how to find the additional money necessary for your goals, through the cash flow statement. You'll also learn where to invest the money to earn the best possible return (diversification of investments). In addition, we'll specifically examine two objectives that will be of concern to many women: managing debt and retirement planning.

But first things first. We've just figured out where we want to go. So now we have to take an honest look at where we are. We can do this by taking an inventory of our assets and liabilities—what we own and what we owe. Once we complete the Inventory Worksheet, we'll use that information to create a Net Worth Statement. I want everyone to go through all the files, drawers, basements, attics, and any other place you can think of, and come up with statements, insurance policies, loan documents, etc., that will assist you in compiling this list. Here's a checklist for help in thinking of items (opposite). If you're not clear on what some of the things are, don't worry—we'll cover the categories in our next session.

SUSAN: Oh boy! This sounds like real fun. What if you have no idea where to look for these documents? I don't think I could find all of them if my life depended on it.

ANN: If you can't find them, how do you expect anyone else to find them if you should become incapacitated? It may not sound like the most excitement you ever had, but believe me, the time spent will be worth it. When filling out the worksheet, you may find that you're missing a document or certain information. Don't panic about it. I realize that pulling this information together is a chore, but better to do this *before* you need it, than when you are desperate.

So, everyone, happy hunting—and on to our assets and liabilities. Reader, now's the time to gather the material that will help you compile this list.

Checklist for Assets and Liabilities

INVESTMENTS
Bank statements
  Checking
  Savings
  CDs
  Other investments
Latest brokerage statements
Latest mutual fund statements
Other investment-related
  documents
Investments held by you at home
  or in a vault (stocks, bonds,
  etc.)

INSURANCE
Personal life insurance statements
Annuity statements
Homeowner's coverage
Personal coverage
  Receipts on large purchases, if
  available

EMPLOYMENT BENEFITS
401(k) statement
Pension statement
Other retirement plan statements
Stock option plan
IRA statement
Keogh statement

OTHER PERSONAL DOCUMENTS
Wills and codicils
Trust documents
  Created by you
  To benefit you
Separation, divorce, alimony,
  child support agreements
Last two pay statements
Rental agreements

LOAN DOCUMENTS AND STATEMENTS
Mortgages
Education loan
Auto loan
Life insurance loan
Equity source loan
Credit card statements
Loans due to you

TANGIBLE ITEMS
Furnishings
Household items
Clothing
Jewelry
Furs
Antiques
Art
Autos
Collections

■■ ■■■ ■ ■■ ■ ■■ ■ ■■ ■ ■■ ■

INVENTORY OF ASSETS AND LIABILITIES

■■ ■■ ■■

ANN: Where are you financially at this very moment? You may feel as if you're swimming against the tide, working harder and harder to stay in the same place—but do you know why? You need to take a picture of your money situation right now to define what you're starting out with today. This information, combined with your Goals list, forms the basis for figuring out how we get from where you are now to where you want to be.

STACY: This worksheet will take me about one minute. I own nothing!

ANN: I'm not so sure. Do you have clothes? A stereo? A TV? Remember, we are talking not only about money or stocks but also about tangible items. They have value and they are counted when we determine our net worth.

CAROL: What about the money I owe on my credit cards? You only mentioned resources.

ANN: Good point. The Inventory Worksheets we'll fill out list our assets (the things we own) *and* our liabilities (the things we owe). Together, they establish our financial profile at this moment.

TERRY: Are monthly bills considered a liability?

CAROL: I don't get that either. Also are my alimony and child support assets?

ANN: Many people are confused about what belongs on the balance sheet. We need to clear up some definitions before we tackle this assignment:

Asset	Everything you own
Liability	Everything you owe

Income   Revenue coming in
Expenses   Revenue going out

We will fully discuss income and expenses in a later chapter. For now, it is important to know that income does *not* show up on our balance sheet of assets unless the money coming in is *transformed into* the ownership of an asset. Similarly, the monthly flow of your expenses is also not on the balance sheet of liabilities unless you're behind on payments. What is stated is a list of all your debts.

So, you would *not* list your monthly mortgage payment of $435, which is part of your monthly expenses, but you *would* list your remaining mortgage debt of $45,000.

Therefore, Carol, do child support and alimony belong on your balance sheet?

CAROL: No. They are income. And I understand also that my normal bills every month are expenses, not liabilities.

ANN: Right.

TERRY: And since I am current on paying my bills, I would show no liabilities on my balance sheet.

ANN: Exactly. Now let's discuss how the next set of worksheets should be approached.

Filling out the first sheet, the inventory of assets and liabilities is important for two reasons. One, it gives you a permanent record of what you own and what you owe, where the asset (or liability) is, when you purchased it, and the current value. Two, the inventory makes it very easy to transfer the totals from each category onto your Net Worth Statement (take the figure from "current market value," the column that is shaded). Use the same date of value for all categories, so that you can present a true picture as of a single day. This means that the price of all stocks, bonds, and mutual funds should be obtained as of the same date. Real estate prices are approximate, so as long as they are current market value, it will be fine. Obtaining a new appraisal of items is not necessary for this exercise, unless the appraisal is outdated.

Now that you've done your homework and gathered all your documentation (household, investments, loans, etc.), create files for each category, so you will have them for future use and for tax documentation. (Some categories can be combined into the same file.)

Before we start, let's look at a blank Inventory Worksheet.

STACY: I don't know what half of these things are!

ANN: Not to worry. Here are some definitions and ideas on how to arrive at the values.

Inventory Worksheet

ASSETS

TYPE OF ACCOUNT	# OF UNITS/ SHARES	DATE ACQUIRED	COST	CURRENT MARKET VALUE	INT./ GROWTH RATE (%)	ANNUAL INT./ GROWTH AMT.	OWNER(S)
LIQUID							
Cash/checking							
Savings							
Money-market funds							
Other							
TOTAL							
INVESTMENTS							
CDs							
TOTAL							
Stocks							
TOTAL							
Bonds							
TOTAL							
Mutual funds							
TOTAL							
EMPLOYMENT RELATED							
Pension/profit shg.							
401(k)							
IRA							
Keogh/SEP							
Business interest							
TOTAL							
PERSONAL PROPERTY							
Furnishings/household							
Autos/boats/RVs							
Jewelry/furs							
Collections							
Other							
TOTAL							

TYPE OF ACCOUNT	# OF UNITS/ SHARES	DATE ACQUIRED	COST	CURRENT MARKET VALUE	INT./ GROWTH RATE (%)	ANNUAL INT./ GROWTH AMT.	OWNER(S)
REAL ESTATE							
Primary home							
Second home							
TOTAL							
Investment properties							
TOTAL							
MISCELLANEOUS ASSETS							
Annuities							
Notes receivable							
Trusts							
Cash value of insurance							
TOTAL							

LIABILITIES

SHORT-TERM					
LENDER	TYPE OF LOAN	BALANCE DUE	INTEREST RATE (%)	ANNUAL INT. AMT. $	SIGNER/CO-SIGNER
Credit card 1					
Credit card 2					
Credit card 3					
Out-of-pocket medical/dental					
Current bills not paid					
TOTAL					

SHORT-TERM		
TAXES DUE	AMOUNT DUE	DATE DUE
Federal		
State		
City		
Self-employment		
TOTAL		

LONG-TERM					
LENDER	TYPE OF LOAN	BALANCE DUE	INTEREST RATE (%)	ANNUAL INT. AMT. $	SIGNER/CO-SIGNER
Mortgage					
Equity source					
Auto					
Education					
Life insurance					
Other					
TOTAL					

ASSETS

Liquid

Include all checking accounts, savings accounts, or currency you might have shoved under the mattress (a savings method I do *not* recommend). Use end-of-the-month statements from your bank.

MONEY-MARKET FUNDS: A mutual fund that invests in short-term high-yield investments that a small investor could not afford to invest in individually. Use liquid statement issued by your bank, broker, or fund to value.

Investments

CERTIFICATES OF DEPOSIT (CD): A bank deposit that earns a specific interest rate for a specific period of time. There is a penalty for early withdrawal. To determine its value, use your *initial* investment amount, not including anticipated interest (just in case you need to withdraw prematurely).

STOCKS: Equity position in a company. For valuing stock positions, use the end-of-the-month statement from your brokerage account, or price the stocks individually, using the financial section of your newspaper. For those prices that are impossible to find, call the broker who sold the stocks to you and ask her to price them.

BONDS: Debt position (meaning money you have *lent*) in a company, government, or municipality. For current value of savings bonds, ask your banker. Many corporate and government bonds are listed in the newspaper. Any you cannot find can be priced by your broker, as can municipal bonds.

MUTUAL FUNDS: A mutual fund is a way for an individual to participate in a professionally managed investment fund by pooling her resources with other investors with a similar objective. A mutual fund can invest in all stocks, all bonds, a combination of stocks and bonds, specific types of stocks, specific types of bonds, etc. You would invest in a mutual fund if you did not want to pick out individual investments but wanted to take advantage of professional management, diversification, and lower transaction fees. I suggest you list each fund you own separately, using the valuation date from your statement.

Employment Related

PENSION/PROFIT SHARING/401(K): Participation in a company plan. It may be contributory (you put in money) or noncontributory (only your firm puts in money), or a combination of both (you contribute and your company matches a certain percentage). Some firms have more than one plan. List each one separately. Also, if you have plans from previous employers, be sure to list these also. (If you have taken the proceeds from the previous plan and rolled them over into a rollover IRA, they will be listed under IRAs.) You should receive a statement on the value of your funds at least once a year (many companies produce this quarterly). If your statement isn't due for some time, ask your employee benefits or personnel department if they can calculate your current share for you.

IRA: An individual retirement account that allows you to contribute $2,000 per year on a tax-deferred basis to an investment program for your retirement. You can take the amount you contribute as a tax deduction if you (or your spouse) don't participate in a retirement plan from work, *or* if you do participate but have adjusted gross income under a certain amount (single $25,000, married $40,000). You can get a partial deduction if you earn more (single up to $35,000, married up to $50,000), but above that amount, there is no deduction unless you have no other retirement plan. List all your IRAs (you can add them together if there are many), including any rollover IRAs (money from plans of previous employers that you have put into a tax-deferred account until at least age $59\frac{1}{2}$, so that you do not have to pay taxes and penalties).

KEOGH/SEP: A retirement plan for the self-employed. If you are or ever were self-employed, or if you have a side business and started a Keogh or a SEP plan, list the current value from the statements.

BUSINESS INTERESTS: If you own any part of a business, whether or not you run it, list your participation. You may be a limited partner and receive some type of distribution each year. The distribution would be income, but the value of your ownership would belong on your Net Worth Statement.

Personal Property

This includes the value of furnishings, household goods, jewelry, furs, antiques, art, autos, etc. The value used for the balance sheet is usually the same as the amount you would use for your household insurance.

Determining these values may necessitate hiring an appraiser. But remember, be conservative in your valuation for the inventory. If you are in the position of *needing* to sell something, you may have to settle for less than its full worth.

Real Estate

I made two categories for real estate—one for your residence and your second home, if any; and the second for investment property. The reason is that usually we don't buy and sell the homes we live in that frequently; however, investment property is just that—used to turn a profit. To determine the value, look for sale prices of comparative properties or hire a real estate appraiser. This does not have to be "to the penny," but it should be realistic.

If you have a real estate limited partnership, use the amount of your original investment, unless you have an updated valuation.

Miscellaneous Assets

This is a catchall for anything I didn't already mention. Like annuities. An annuity is a contract between a life insurance company and an individual. The individual pays a lump sum payment or periodic payments to the insurance company, and the insurance company agrees to pay out at retirement a fixed (or variable) amount of money over the individual's lifetime or for a specific period of time.

Does anyone owe you money? This is a note receivable, and should also be listed in this category.

Another miscellaneous asset is a trust of which you are the beneficiary. You may be receiving payments currently, but if you will not acquire assets until a future date, list it. However, do not include this figure when we transfer data to the Net Worth Statement, because you are not in current possession.

INSURANCE: List all policies on a separate page and attach to your inventory so that you will have a record of the details. However, for the purposes of your Net Worth Statement, the only figure that will show up is from life insurance that has a cash surrender value (whole, universal, or permanent policies). Check your policy's cash surrender value chart to find your current cash value, or call your agent to get it for you.

You'll be happy to know the list of liabilities is considerably shorter than the list of assets.

LIABILITIES

We break liabilities down into short-term (currently owed) and long-term (loans paid over a long period of time, such as home, car, education).

Short-term

This would include credit card balances, medical and dental bills, the current payment due on a long term loan, and any outstanding debts for which you are behind in payment. If you have estimated taxes due (other than the amount with-held from your paycheck) or unpaid capital gains, this would also be listed.

Long-term

Any loans that you have contracted to pay over a long period of time should be listed, which would include home, car, furniture, education. You may also have a personal loan from a bank or an individual, which would be termed a note pay-able. If you have borrowed against your life insurance, this, too, should be noted.

I know this is a lot to digest at once. I suggest you do the following: Take the time you need (but not too long, we don't want to lose momentum) and fill out your inventory list (reader, use the blank on pp. 22–23). If you want to see how the others filled out their sheets, turn to the next lesson first. If you're not clear on what a category is (such as what is a trust?) leave that section blank. Chances are, if you don't know what it is, you don't own it. Once you have been through the sheets once, look up all the items you have questions on in the glossary in the back of this book.

LESSON 5

▬▬ ▬▬ ▬▬ ▬▬ ▬▬ ▬▬ ▬▬ ▬▬ ▬▬ ▬▬ ▬▬ ▬▬ ▬▬ ▬▬ ▬▬

INVENTORY REVISITED

▬▬▬ ▬▬ ▬▬▬

ANN: I can't wait to see your Inventory Worksheets. How did everyone do?

STACY: I was wrong about its taking me one minute. It actually took me 15 minutes, because I couldn't decide what my tangible property was worth. It did make me think about all the blanks though, and how much I would like to fill them in. I can't wait to have a full-time job, so I can be eligible for the 401(k) plan.

TERRY: Can I tell you this great thing that happened to me? Since my husband has always handled the finances, I had to approach him to help me fill out the inventory. When I explained the process I was learning and discussed my goals with him, he looked so relieved! I always felt he didn't want me to know, but the truth was he thought I had no interest. We sat down and worked on the sheets together, and for the first time I honestly feel like an equal partner. And he feels better also—being a police officer makes him especially concerned about our family's security.

CAROL: I should have done this *before* my divorce. I'm sure my settlement would have been substantially higher if I knew all of our assets. But after I received the proceeds of our divorce settlement, it was very clear to me what my assets are. The unnerving part of this exercise to me was listing all my debts! The mortgage and the car loan are OK, but I'm really concerned about the credit card debt.

JANE: When my husband died, I received $100,000 in insurance money. I also got his pension, which I rolled over for my own retirement. There was one stock certificate, which I found in the vault that my husband bought years ago. I don't know if it has any value. Additionally, I have been diligent about putting money in my 401(k) plan, and I will have a small pension from my firm. I have the house we bought 25 years ago, but I still owe $25,000 on the home improvement loan we took out 6 years ago. I must say, I impressed myself that I was able to put the inventory together and feel I have a handle on this part of the project.

TERRY: You know, Jane, it seems to me you are very organized. In your circumstances, I wouldn't have had a clue as to what I owned.

JANE: You should have seen me when Bill died. I didn't even know if he had any life insurance or what investments we had. So, as I said, I put everything not already invested into the bank. I now finally feel ready to take the next step. I'm sure I can earn more on the money, but I'm afraid to lose any money.

Susan, I'm curious how you made out since you were nervous about this assignment.

SUSAN: Well, I knew this would be very difficult for me, and I was right. Nothing was where I thought it was. I found my mortgage papers after a frantic search. You'll never guess where they were. In my lingerie drawer! Why?—I have no idea. I had no documentation from my pension plan and my 401(k) at work, but the employee benefit people gave me copies. I did find a lot of receipts for objects I had bought over the years, and I also came across the note my brother signed when I lent him $25,000 for the down payment on his house. It was a struggle, but I *do* feel I have accomplished something.

ANN: I'm so glad. I was concerned about you, Susan, but knew you would come through. It sounds to me like you all learned something about yourselves as well as about your assets and liabilities.

Stacy's worksheet is on pp. 30–31, Terry's is on pp. 32–33, Carol's is on pp. 34–35, Jane's is on pp. 36–37, and Susan's is on pp. 38–39.

Inventory Worksheet

ASSETS

TYPE OF ACCOUNT	# OF UNITS/ SHARES	DATE ACQUIRED	COST	CURRENT MARKET VALUE	INT./ GROWTH RATE (%)	ANNUAL INT./ GROWTH AMT.	OWNER(S)
LIQUID							
Cash/checking			500	500	0%	—	Self
Savings							
Money-market funds							
Other							
		TOTAL	500	500		0	
INVESTMENTS							
CDs							
		TOTAL					
Stocks							
		TOTAL					
Bonds							
		TOTAL					
Mutual funds							
		TOTAL					
EMPLOYMENT RELATED							
Pension/profit shg.							
401(k)							
IRA							
Keogh/SEP							
Business interest							
		TOTAL					
PERSONAL PROPERTY							
Furnishings/household	(Clothing)		1500	1000	—	—	Self
Autos/boats/RVs							
Jewelry/furs			gifts	1200	—	—	Self
Collections (ROCK MEMORABILIA)			300	800	—	—	Self
Other							
		TOTAL	1800	3000	—		

TYPE OF ACCOUNT	# OF UNITS/ SHARES	DATE ACQUIRED	COST	CURRENT MARKET VALUE	INT./ GROWTH RATE (%)	ANNUAL INT./ GROWTH AMT.	OWNER(S)
REAL ESTATE							
Primary home							
Second home							
TOTAL							
Investment properties							
TOTAL							
MISCELLANEOUS ASSETS							
Annuities							
Notes receivable							
Trusts							
Cash value of insurance							
TOTAL							

LIABILITIES

SHORT-TERM

LENDER	TYPE OF LOAN	BALANCE DUE	INTEREST RATE (%)	ANNUAL INT. AMT. $	SIGNER/CO-SIGNER
Credit card 1					
Credit card 2					
Credit card 3					
Out-of-pocket medical/dental					
Current bills not paid					
TOTAL					

SHORT-TERM

TAXES DUE	AMOUNT DUE	DATE DUE
Federal		
State		
City		
Self-employment		
TOTAL		

LONG-TERM

LENDER	TYPE OF LOAN	BALANCE DUE	INTEREST RATE (%)	ANNUAL INT. AMT. $	SIGNER/CO-SIGNER
Mortgage					
Equity source					
Auto					
Education					
Life insurance					
Other LOAN From Parents	Personal	1300	0%	—	
TOTAL		1300			

Inventory Worksheet

ASSETS   TERRY

TYPE OF ACCOUNT	# OF UNITS/ SHARES	DATE ACQUIRED	COST	CURRENT MARKET VALUE	INT./ GROWTH RATE (%)	ANNUAL INT./ GROWTH AMT.	OWNER(S)
LIQUID							
Cash/checking			500	500	0%	—	joint
Savings			1000	1000	3%	30	joint
Money-market funds *Ready Assets*			750	750	4%	30	joint
Other							
		TOTAL	2250	2250		60	
INVESTMENTS							
CDs							
		TOTAL					
Stocks							
		TOTAL					
Bonds							
		TOTAL					
Mutual funds							
		TOTAL					
EMPLOYMENT RELATED							
Pension/profit shg.		Since 1980	—	32,000	6	1920	husband
401(k)							
IRA							
Keogh/SEP							
Business interest							
		TOTAL		32,000		1920	
PERSONAL PROPERTY							
Furnishings/household			5000	2500			
Autos/boats/RVs		1985 1989	8000	1000			
Jewelry/furs							
Collections							
Other							
		TOTAL	13,000	3500			

TYPE OF ACCOUNT	# OF UNITS/ SHARES	DATE ACQUIRED	COST	CURRENT MARKET VALUE	INT./ GROWTH RATE (%)	ANNUAL INT./ GROWTH AMT.	OWNER(S)
REAL ESTATE							
Primary home							
Second home							
		TOTAL					
Investment properties							
		TOTAL					
MISCELLANEOUS ASSETS							
Annuities							
Notes receivable							
Trusts							
Cash value of insurance		3/1/86		1500	5%	by schedule of insurance	husband
		TOTAL		1500			

LIABILITIES

SHORT-TERM					
LENDER	TYPE OF LOAN	BALANCE DUE	INTEREST RATE (%)	ANNUAL INT. AMT. $	SIGNER/CO-SIGNER
Credit card 1 *Revolving Credit*		625	16%	100	husband
Credit card 2					
Credit card 3					
Out-of-pocket medical/dental					
Current bills not paid					
TOTAL		625		100	

SHORT-TERM		
TAXES DUE	AMOUNT DUE	DATE DUE
Federal		
State		
City		
Self-employment		
TOTAL		

LONG-TERM					
LENDER	TYPE OF LOAN	BALANCE DUE	INTEREST RATE (%)	ANNUAL INT. AMT. $	SIGNER/CO-SIGNER
Mortgage					
Equity source					
Auto					
Education					
Life insurance					
Other					
TOTAL					

Inventory Worksheet

ASSETS   CAROL

TYPE OF ACCOUNT	# OF UNITS/ SHARES	DATE ACQUIRED	COST	CURRENT MARKET VALUE	INT./ GROWTH RATE (%)	ANNUAL INT./ GROWTH AMT.	OWNER(S)
LIQUID							
Cash/checking			500	500	0%		Self
Savings							
Money-market funds							
Other							
		TOTAL	500	500			
INVESTMENTS							
CDs		1/15/90	3000	3932	7	210	Self
		TOTAL		3932		210	
Stocks							
		TOTAL					
Bonds							
		TOTAL					
Mutual funds							
		TOTAL					
EMPLOYMENT RELATED							
Pension/profit shg.							
401(k)							
IRA		various	6000	8200	8	656	Self
Keogh/SEP							
Business interest							
		TOTAL		8200			
PERSONAL PROPERTY							
Furnishings/household			7000	5000	—	—	Self
Autos/boats/RVs		1991	10,000	5000	—	—	Self
Jewelry/furs							
Collections		various	2500	1500	—	—	Self
Other							
		TOTAL	19,500	11,500			

TYPE OF ACCOUNT	# OF UNITS/ SHARES	DATE ACQUIRED	COST	CURRENT MARKET VALUE	INT./ GROWTH RATE (%)	ANNUAL INT./ GROWTH AMT.	OWNER(S)
REAL ESTATE							
Primary home		1985	95,000	110,000	?		Self
Second home							
		TOTAL	95,000	110,000			
Investment properties							
		TOTAL					
MISCELLANEOUS ASSETS							
Annuities							
Notes receivable							
Trusts							
Cash value of insurance							
		TOTAL					

LIABILITIES

SHORT-TERM					
LENDER	TYPE OF LOAN	BALANCE DUE	INTEREST RATE (%)	ANNUAL INT. AMT. $	SIGNER/CO-SIGNER
Credit card 1	gas	1500	16%	240	Self
Credit card 2	Dept. Store	2000	18%	360	Self
Credit card 3	Nt'l Charge	5000	18%	900	Self
Out-of-pocket medical/dental					
Current bills not paid					
	TOTAL	8500		1500	

SHORT-TERM		
TAXES DUE	AMOUNT DUE	DATE DUE
Federal		
State		
City		
Self-employment		
TOTAL		

LONG-TERM					
LENDER	TYPE OF LOAN	BALANCE DUE	INTEREST RATE (%)	ANNUAL INT. AMT. $	SIGNER/CO-SIGNER
Mortgage refinanced 1992	30yr. fixed	50,000	8½%	4600 Int. + principal	Self
Equity source					
Auto	Auto/2yr.	2,500	10%	250	Self
Education					
Life insurance					
Other Parents	Personal	2,500	0%	—	Self
	TOTAL	55,000		4850	

Inventory Worksheet

ASSETS JANE

TYPE OF ACCOUNT	# OF UNITS/ SHARES	DATE ACQUIRED	COST	CURRENT MARKET VALUE	INT./ GROWTH RATE (%)	ANNUAL INT./ GROWTH AMT.	OWNER(S)
LIQUID							
Cash/checking			2000	2000	2%	40	Self
Savings		1991	125,000	150,000	5%	7500	Self
Money-market funds							
Other							
		TOTAL	127,000	152,000		7540	
INVESTMENTS							
CDs							
		TOTAL					
Stocks							
XYZ Company	100	5/6/71	?	?	—	—	Husband
		TOTAL					
Bonds							
		TOTAL					
Mutual funds							
		TOTAL					
EMPLOYMENT RELATED							
Pension/profit shg.			—	125,000		4800	Self
401(k)		Since 1970	23,000	75,000	8	6000	Self
IRA		Various	20,000	60,000	8	4800	Self
Keogh/SEP							
Business interest							
		TOTAL	43,000	260,000		15,600	
PERSONAL PROPERTY							
Furnishings/household		Various	12,500	10,000	—	—	Self
Autos/boats/RVs		1991	11,500	7,000	—	—	Self
Jewelry/furs		Various	5,000	9,000	—	—	Self
Collections		Various	4,000	10,000			Self
Other							
		TOTAL	33,000	36,000			

TYPE OF ACCOUNT	# OF UNITS/ SHARES	DATE ACQUIRED	COST	CURRENT MARKET VALUE	INT./ GROWTH RATE (%)	ANNUAL INT./ GROWTH AMT.	OWNER(S)
REAL ESTATE							
Primary home		1965	60,000	260,000	?		Self
Second home							
		TOTAL	60,000	260,000			
Investment properties							
		TOTAL					
MISCELLANEOUS ASSETS							
Annuities							
Notes receivable							
Trusts							
Cash value of insurance							
		TOTAL					

LIABILITIES

SHORT-TERM

LENDER	TYPE OF LOAN	BALANCE DUE	INTEREST RATE (%)	ANNUAL INT. AMT. $	SIGNER/CO-SIGNER
Credit card 1					
Credit card 2					
Credit card 3					
Out-of-pocket medical/dental					
Current bills not paid					
	TOTAL				

SHORT-TERM

TAXES DUE	AMOUNT DUE	DATE DUE
Federal 2nd qtr. estimate	500	June 15
State 2nd qtr. estimate	150	June 15
City		
Self-employment		
TOTAL	650	

LONG-TERM

LENDER	TYPE OF LOAN	BALANCE DUE	INTEREST RATE (%)	ANNUAL INT. AMT. $	SIGNER/CO-SIGNER
Mortgage					
Equity source	Home Improvement	25,000	10	2500	Self
Auto					
Education					
Life insurance					
Other					
	TOTAL	25,000			

Inventory Worksheet

ASSETS   SUSAN

TYPE OF ACCOUNT	# OF UNITS/ SHARES	DATE ACQUIRED	COST	CURRENT MARKET VALUE	INT./ GROWTH RATE (%)	ANNUAL INT./ GROWTH AMT.	OWNER(S)
LIQUID							
Cash/checking			2500	2500	2%	50	Self
Savings							
Money-market funds							
Other							
TOTAL			2500	2500		50	
INVESTMENTS							
CDs							
TOTAL							
Stocks							
TOTAL							
Bonds							
TOTAL							
Mutual funds							
Bond fund		6/90	4500	5680	6%	340	Self
TOTAL			4500	5680		340	
EMPLOYMENT RELATED							
(Pension/profit shg.)				90,000	by formula		
401(k)		Began 1983	48,000	91,120	6	4800	Self
IRA		1983-1986	6,000	12,800	10	1200	Self
Keogh/SEP							
Business interest							
TOTAL			54,000	193,920		6,000	
PERSONAL PROPERTY							
Furnishings/(household)		Various	35,000	20,000			
Autos/boats/RVs							
Jewelry/furs		"	17,500	10,000			
Collections *Furniture*		1989-present	2500	3500			
Other							
TOTAL			55,000	33,500			

TYPE OF ACCOUNT	# OF UNITS/ SHARES	DATE ACQUIRED	COST	CURRENT MARKET VALUE	INT./ GROWTH RATE (%)	ANNUAL INT./ GROWTH AMT.	OWNER(S)
REAL ESTATE							
Primary home		1988	100,000	175,000			Self
Second home							
		TOTAL	100,000	175,000			
Investment properties							
		TOTAL					
MISCELLANEOUS ASSETS							
Annuities							
Notes receivable *Brother*		1990	25,000	25,000	0%		Self
Trusts							
Cash value of insurance							
		TOTAL	25,000	25,000			

LIABILITIES

SHORT-TERM					
LENDER	TYPE OF LOAN	BALANCE DUE	INTEREST RATE (%)	ANNUAL INT. AMT. $	SIGNER/CO-SIGNER
Credit card 1	Revolving Debt.	1500	16%	240	Self
Credit card 2	Nat'l Card	1000	14%	140	Self
Credit card 3					
Out-of-pocket medical/dental					
Current bills not paid					
TOTAL		2500		380	

SHORT-TERM		
TAXES DUE	AMOUNT DUE	DATE DUE
Federal		
State		
City		
Self-employment		
TOTAL		

LONG-TERM					
LENDER	TYPE OF LOAN	BALANCE DUE	INTEREST RATE (%)	ANNUAL INT. AMT. $	SIGNER/CO-SIGNER
Mortgage	15 yr. fixed	75,000	10 1/2%	13,272	Self
Equity source				Int. + Principal	
Auto					
Education					
Life insurance					
Other					
TOTAL		75,000		13,272	

LESSON 6

■■ ■ ■■ ■ ■■ ■ ■ ■■ ■■ ■ ■ ■■ ■ ■■ ■ ■ ■■ ■ ■■ ■ ■■ ■ ■ ■■ ■

NET WORTH

■■ ■■ ■

ANN: You did such a good job on your inventories that your Net Worth Statements will take you very little time. The concept of how we figure out our net worth is very simple: Use your Inventory Worksheets for the current value of all your assets and the cost of all your liabilities. The difference between your assets and liabilities is your net worth. Obviously, this number changes every time you add to your assets or increase your liabilities. This is why you should compute your net worth every year. Remember, your Net Worth Statement (otherwise known as a balance sheet) is a picture of your financial condition on one given date. Our goal is to have a greater net worth every year.

Reader, have a look at how Susan compiled hers (opposite), and then fill out your own (p. 42).

You now each have a Net Worth Statement, which forms a basis for comparison each year when you recalculate it. However, there are actually many other reasons to have a Net Worth Statement. Bankers will require it if you want a loan to finance a home or a business. Insurance agents will want to look at it to help you determine the need for life insurance and disability insurance. It will assist you and your lawyer when you make your estate plan and determine what you will pass on to your heirs, and it will help you and any financial advisors calculate if you have accumulated enough for a comfortable retirement.

The balance sheet is a tool for making adjustments. If you have most of your assets in real estate, which at times can be difficult to sell and convert to cash quickly, you may determine that you need more investments that produce income or that could be sold more easily. If most of your money is in cash or savings accounts, perhaps you should try more long-term investments that will give you a better return. If you have a lot of debt, you can develop a program to lessen the

Net Worth Worksheet

ASSETS		LIABILITIES	
LIQUID		**SHORT-TERM**	
Cash/checking	2500	Credit cards	2500
Savings		Out-of-pocket	
Money market funds		medical/dental	
Other		Unpaid bills	
TOTAL **2500**		Taxes due	
INVESTMENTS		Other	
CDs		TOTAL **2500**	
Stocks		**LONG-TERM**	
Bonds		Mortgage/equity source	75,000
Mutual funds *(Bond fund)*	5,680	Auto	
TOTAL **5,680**		Education	
EMPLOYMENT RELATED		Life insurance	
Pension/profit shg.	90,000	Notes payable	
401(k)	91,120	Other	
IRA	12,800	TOTAL **75,000**	
Keogh/SEP			
Business interest		TOTAL LIABILITIES **77,500**	
TOTAL **193,920**			
PERSONAL PROPERTY			
Furnishings/household	20,000		
Autos/boats/RVs	—		
Jewelry/furs	10,000		
Collections *Furniture*	3,500		
Other			
TOTAL **33,500**			
REAL ESTATE			
Primary home	175,000		
Second home			
Invest. prop.			
Invest. prop.			
TOTAL **175,000**			
MISCELLANEOUS ASSETS			
Annuities			
Notes receivable	25,000		
Cash value of insurance			
TOTAL **25,000**			
TOTAL ASSETS: **435,600**		**NET WORTH** **358,100**	

Net Worth Worksheet

DATE _____

ASSETS

LIQUID
Cash/checking   _____
Savings   _____
Money market funds   _____
Other   _____
    TOTAL _____

INVESTMENTS
CDs   _____
Stocks   _____
Bonds   _____
Mutual funds   _____
    TOTAL _____

EMPLOYMENT RELATED
Pension/profit shg.   _____
401(k)   _____
IRA   _____
Keogh/SEP   _____
Business interest   _____
    TOTAL _____

PERSONAL PROPERTY
Furnishings/household _____
Autos/boats/RVs   _____
Jewelry/furs   _____
Collections   _____
Other   _____
    TOTAL _____

REAL ESTATE
Primary home   _____
Second home   _____
Invest. prop.   _____
Invest. prop.   _____
    TOTAL _____

MISCELLANEOUS ASSETS
Annuities   _____
Notes receivable   _____
Cash value of insurance _____
    TOTAL _____

TOTAL ASSETS: _____

LIABILITIES

SHORT-TERM
Credit cards   _____
Out-of-pocket
   medical/dental   _____
Unpaid bills   _____
Taxes due   _____
Other   _____
    TOTAL _____

LONG-TERM
Mortgage/equity source   _____
Auto   _____
Education   _____
Life insurance   _____
Notes payable   _____
Other   _____
    TOTAL _____
TOTAL LIABILITIES _____

NET WORTH _____

burden. Many times we sense something is wrong. But only when we see our assets and liabilities written before us will it be clear what steps we need to take.

SUSAN: When I was transferring my assets and liabilities to the Net Worth Statement I had no idea where a lot of what I made over the past 15 years went.

ANN: You're not alone. It's been said there are only two ways to spend money. Most of us spend it in the first way: on things that depreciate, get thrown away, or fade from memory. Examples? Depreciation would be the new car you have wanted for so long. The minute you drive it off the lot, it has depreciated thousands of dollars. Thrown away would be all those clothes that "spoke" to us through the window of the department store. We bought them, and next season they were too long, too short, we lost five pounds, we gained five pounds, etc., and we tossed them. And faded from memory is that wonderful dinner or that fabulous vacation. Important, but not lasting. There is, however, another way to spend money. And that is on things that *appreciate.* Things that not only stay with us as we age, but also generally increase in value, such as a home, an education, a retirement fund. If we put our money into items that appreciate, not only will our balance sheets look healthier but our lives will also be enriched.

TERRY: That's easier said than done. I have three children and a mess of monthly bills, and all I know is the money is gone before I have even had a chance to think about where to put it.

ANN: We all are in the same boat. Our circumstances are different, but the bottom line is that most of us live right up to the amount of money we make, and in many cases, right beyond it, causing anxiety. Spending money clearly is much easier than saving it. So let's *continue* to spend money—but on the items we have set as goals. Any thoughts on how to do this?

JANE: When my husband and I were first married, we found we never had any money left over to go on vacation. One year, I began taking the change from my purse and the change from his pants pockets every day and putting it into a big jar. Each day we started fresh with no coins, and at the end of the month, we would wrap and deposit them into an account. At the end of the year we had enough money to go on vacation.

ANN: Jane, what you were doing was setting up a system to create the funds you wanted to achieve your goal of a vacation. Which is the essence of what we're going to do for *all* the priority items we have on our list of goals.

Since it is not going to be possible to accomplish all of our objectives using pocket change, we need to develop a system that will help us to identify where the money is coming from (income) and where it is being spent (outgo). Let's break now and pick up this conversation at our next session.

LESSON 7

▪▪▪—▪—▪▪▪—▪—▪—▪▪▪—▪—▪—▪▪▪—▪—▪▪▪—▪—▪—▪▪▪—▪—▪—

CASH FLOW

▬▬ ▪▪ ▬▬

CAROL: As I understand it, there are only two choices when it comes to making sure your cash flow is positive. Either make more money or spend less.

ANN: Well put. Of course, we would love to be able to make more money, and maybe this is an option. If you are not working, seek part-time or full-time employment. If you need to be home, think of a business you can start there. If you are working, think of ways to improve your position and your income. Earning money empowers you to make positive decisions about your life and the lives of your family.

The other side of the coin is to spend less. You may not think this is possible, but let's see. Susan, do you eat lunch every day?

SUSAN: Of course I do.

ANN: What do you think you spend on lunch?

SUSAN: Sometimes I go to business lunches that my firm pays for, but most of the time I order in or go out and spend between $5 and $10, I guess.

ANN: Do you agree that if you brought your lunch from home the same meal would cost you much less?

SUSAN: No question. But I don't have the time in the morning to make myself lunch. Besides, it's such a hassle.

ANN: A highly motivated person with a reason to save $20 to $40 a week might not mind preparing her lunch the night before or getting up 10 minutes earlier if she knew it would mean an additional $1,000 to $2,000 per year to pay for something more important to her.

STACY: As much as $2,000! I'm going to bring my muffin in from home from now on and drink the coffee they make at the office. That would save me at least $1.50 a day.

ANN: Right. We need to think about the things we do every day that have become habits and analyze which of them are really important, and which of them we do without thinking about it. I am not in the business of changing your life-style if you don't want to change. But I want you to know what your life-style *is*. That way, *you* decide exactly where to spend your money, rather than just going along as usual. It is a conscious decision.

Let me give you an example. As you know, I live in New York City, where people take cabs frequently, even though we have a very extensive public transportation system. I was leaving my office one day and saw a woman who had taken one of my seminars hailing a cab. I caught her eye and smiled. As soon as she saw me, she hopped on a bus that was conveniently waiting there, looked out the window at me, and waved.

I have to tell you I felt great because I know I saved that person a few dollars. You see, before she saw me she was getting into a cab because she had always done that before. As soon as she saw me, she realized she had an alternative. If it helps you to think of me sitting on your shoulder when you are about to make a purchase, do it. If you still buy whatever it is, then you truly want it.

TERRY: I can't think of things that I buy from habit. How can I come up with a list?

ANN: Here is a system that is quite simple and requires paying attention for about a month. Keep a small notebook with you at all times. Jot down the amount you spend in cash every day. You must do this a few times during the day or you'll forget the items you have purchased. For instance:

Bought coffee and muffin on the way to work	$3.00
Stopped to buy a newspaper and a magazine	2.50
Lunch	6.00
Snack	1.00
Ran my stockings, had to buy a pair	2.50
Bought birthday card for my sister	1.50
Snack late afternoon	1.00
Wrapping paper for gift	2.00
Met friends for drink after work	3.00
Stopped at corner grocery for milk and bread	4.00
Rented a movie	2.00
	$28.50

Notice that I rounded all the numbers up. It is much easier to log whole numbers—and we want to be sure to keep the paperwork down to a minimum. If you do this exercise for a month, you'll see why you're always at the cash machine.

SUSAN: Ugh! Track every dollar I spend! This means I have to "be good" every day. Isn't there any other way to come up with the money?

ANN: Sure there is. There is always more than one way to do anything in this world. Here's one way: Some people think it's wonderful to get a tax refund at the end of the year. It's a way of forced savings. You would be smarter to adjust the withholding on your W-4 form at work and put the additional money into your own account. You would earn interest *and* be able to use the money in case of an emergency, rather than wait an entire year for your refund.

Other people find that tracking their cash purchases lets them make painless adjustments—ones that don't change their life-styles and help them accomplish their goals. If this does not work for you, you have many other options. That is the value of analyzing your cash flow and then setting up a budget that fits how you live. Before we can discuss the areas where cutbacks are possible, we need to learn about cash flow statements.

A cash flow statement is not a budget; it is a picture of how much money you earn and where you're spending your money right now. So there's no wishful thinking on the income side such as "I expect to get a bonus next month, so I will include it." We are dealing with what *is*. Similarly, we want a true accounting of what you spend, not what you *think* you *should* spend on clothing, eating out, etc.

Here are the steps in filling one out (see pp. 50–52 for what it looks like):

STEP 1

Start with the income side of the Cash Flow Worksheet. People usually have a very good feel for how much money they earn. If you have any doubts, take your W-2 forms, or use last year's tax return. Add all income and fill in the Total Income line at the end of this section of the worksheet.

STEP 2

Now turn to the expenses. There are some expenses that are the same every month. Take out your checkbook and fill in the items you pay *every month* such as the rent or mortgage, telephone, utilities, etc. Though the telephone and electric bills may not be the same every month, you can average to find the approximate costs. Be sure to include in the *fixed expense* section the amount you will be putting into your emergency fund.

STEP 3

There are many expenses you do not make every month, such as insurance payments, property taxes, doctor bills. Look through your checkbook for these payments and add them to your list.

STEP 4

Here comes the hard part. All the items you have not filled in yet are discretionary, or flexible expenses. We make them haphazardly throughout the year, so they are hard to track. In addition to your checkbook, take out all credit card statements and the log of cash spending you have been doing for the month, and to the best of your ability estimate what you spent this past year on items such as clothing, dinners out, gifts, etc. I know from experience that you will underestimate these—we all do. Don't worry about it, we'll adjust our numbers when we track it monthly on our budgets. For now we just want to be close, not exact.

STEP 5

Once you have totaled each category, note whether it is a fixed or flexible category. Fixed expenses are those you must make every month no matter what happens (such as rent, utilities, insurance). Flexible expenses are those over which you have some control (such as clothing, entertainment, and vacations). Add up all the fixed expenses. Then add up the flexible expenses. Put the totals in the proper line at the end of the worksheet. Subtract the expenses from the income and you will discover the net year-end cash available or the cash shortfall you have each year.

Any questions before you begin?

STACY: I notice from looking at the cash flow sheets that you list health club expenses as flexible. To me, this is fixed. I can't live without working out.

SUSAN: I feel the same way about my housekeeper. My hours at work are too demanding not to have help with my home.

ANN: No problem. I offer this Cash Flow Worksheet as a guideline. You can adjust it as you see fit. And it's important that you are honest about your spending habits so that you have a clear idea of the "flow" of your money.

JANE: Do we include the expenses we don't pay for? For example, I have medical insurance, but my company pays for it.

ANN: You include only the amount you pay for. Many medical plans are paid for by corporations totally; others pay for part and the employee pays for part. Note, however, that what the corporation pays takes care only of the cost of the insurance. When you get to the medical expenses part of the sheet, you should list your out-of-pocket expenses. For example, if you have a $250 deductible, and then pay 20 percent of your expenses up to $2,000, you might list the deductible ($250) plus any amount of the $2,000 you spent in the previous year. If you know you are having surgery and will have to spend the $2,000, list that.

TERRY: Since I have never done anything like this before, I'm not sure my figures are going to be accurate. How valid is this exercise when it might be so imprecise?

ANN: Sometimes it becomes more valuable when you realize how out of touch you've been with your expenses. It will make you pay much closer attention.

Many have had success with this approach: Work on these sheets in pencil so you can make changes. Do the best you can to estimate what you spend in each category, and then make revisions when needed. Round up the annual amounts for easier adding. If, when you add up your fixed and flexible expenses and subtract them from your income, you find that you spend more than you earn, you clearly need to look at the discretionary categories for areas where you can cut down. If you have money left over, yet you have no idea where it is, you have probably underestimated some of your expenses, so go over the list one more time to try to discover what you missed. I suggest you take the next week to work on this, and when you come back for the next session, we'll try to clear up any problems you had.

Reader, your blank Cash Flow Worksheet (pp. 53–55) follows Terry's. Before you begin with your sheet, let's go over just the housing section of Terry's expenses, so you will be clear on how to do yours.

Terry spends $550 per month on rent, which is $6,600 per year (550 times 12). Her utilities cost her $50 per month or $600 per year, and her telephone is $40 per month or $480 per year. These three fixed expenses total $7,680 per year.

Her flexible housing expenses include $500 for household repairs, which are an estimate for the year; and $20 per month, or $240 annually, for cable TV. The flexible costs total $740 for the year.

Total housing costs are $7,680 plus $740 or $8,420. When you are adding all your expenses together, the $7,680 will be part of your total fixed expenses, and the $740 will be part of your total flexible expenses.

Each subsequent category should be approached the same way.

Cash Flow Worksheet

TERRY

DATES: **1/1/94** to **12/31/94**

INCOME	ANNUAL AMOUNT	TOTAL
Gross salary/self-employment income		
Spouse's salary/self-employment income	44,300	
Bonus		
Social Security income		
Pension income		
Alimony/child support		
Interest/dividends	60	
Rental income		
Sale of securities		
Other (specify)		44,360

EXPENSES	MONTHLY AVERAGE	ANNUAL AMOUNT	ANNUAL TOTAL
HOUSING (FIXED)			
Rent/maintenance	550	6600	
Mortgage			
Property taxes			
Utilities (gas, oil, elec., water)	50	600	
Telephone	40	480	7680
HOUSING (FLEXIBLE)			
Household purchases			
Household repairs		500	
Household help			
Cable TV	20	240	
Other			740
EMERGENCY FUND (FIXED)			
Emergency fund			
Goal 1			
Goal 2			
Goal 3			
FOOD (FLEXIBLE)			
Groceries/cleaning supplies	433	5200	
Lunches/snacks	85	1020	6220

(1)

EXPENSES	MONTHLY AVERAGE	ANNUAL AMOUNT	ANNUAL TOTAL
INSURANCE PREMIUMS (FIXED)			
Life *(husband whole life)*		620	
Disability *(husband gets at work)*			
Medical *(husband gets at work)*			
Property and liability		100	
Auto		1300	
Other			
			2020
TRANSPORTATION (FLEXIBLE)			
Car			
Gas/oil		600	
Repairs/maintenance		750	
Rental/loan/lease payments			
Garage/parking/tolls		100	
Public transportation/taxis			
			1450
PERSONAL (FLEXIBLE)			
Clothing		4000	
Cleaning/laundry/shoe repair	33	400	
Beauty shop			
Toiletries/cosmetics	40	500	
Gifts		2500	
Contributions		200	
Pet expenses		150	
			7750
MEDICAL (FLEXIBLE)			
Doctors/therapist		800	
Dentist		320	
Medication/eyeglasses		150	
			1270
EDUCATION (FLEXIBLE)			
Tuition			
Books/supplies/other		300	
Children's activities (camp, lessons, allowances, etc.)		1750	
			2050
ENTERTAINMENT (FLEXIBLE)			
Vacations/weekends away		2500	
Movies/theater/VCR rentals	33	400	

(2)

EXPENSES	MONTHLY AVERAGE	ANNUAL AMOUNT	ANNUAL TOTAL
ENTERTAINMENT (CONTINUED)			
Books/magazines/newspapers	18	220	
Health club/dues			
Sports/hobbies		300	
Dining out	175	2100	
Parties		400	
Wine/liquor	58	700	
(Baby)/pet/house sitters	50	600	
Other			7420
TAXES (FIXED)			
Federal	333	4000	
State/city	115	1400	
Other (unincorporated business tax, etc.)			
Social Security	283	3400	8800
OTHER (FIXED)			
Alimony/child support			
Child care			
Business expense			
Education loans			
Home improvement loans			
Personal loans			
Other (credit cards, etc.)		100	100
OTHER (FLEXIBLE)			
Durable purchases (car, boat, etc.)			
Fees (tax, legal, financial, etc.)		150	150
CAPITAL EXPENDITURES (FLEXIBLE)			
401(k)/retirement plan			
IRA/Keogh/SEP			
Real estate investment			
Other investments			

(3)

TOTAL INCOME $ 44,360

TOTAL FIXED EXPENSES $ 18,600   } 45,950

TOTAL FLEXIBLE EXPENSES $ 27,350

NET YEAR END CASH (SHORTFALL) $ (1,590)

Cash Flow Worksheet

DATES: _____ to _____

INCOME	ANNUAL AMOUNT	TOTAL
Gross salary/self-employment income	_____	
Spouse's salary/self-employment income	_____	
Bonus	_____	
Social Security income	_____	
Pension income	_____	
Alimony/child support	_____	
Interest/dividends	_____	
Rental income	_____	
Sale of securities	_____	
Other (specify)	_____	
		_____

EXPENSES	MONTHLY AVERAGE	ANNUAL AMOUNT	ANNUAL TOTAL
HOUSING (FIXED)			
Rent/maintenance	_____	_____	
Mortgage	_____	_____	
Property taxes	_____	_____	
Utilities (gas, oil, elec., water)	_____	_____	
Telephone	_____	_____	
			_____
HOUSING (FLEXIBLE)			
Household purchases	_____	_____	
Household repairs	_____	_____	
Household help	_____	_____	
Cable TV	_____	_____	
Other	_____	_____	
			_____
EMERGENCY FUND (FIXED)			
Emergency fund	_____	_____	
Goal 1	_____	_____	
Goal 2	_____	_____	
Goal 3	_____	_____	
			_____
FOOD (FLEXIBLE)			
Groceries/cleaning supplies	_____	_____	
Lunches/snacks	_____	_____	
			_____

(1)

EXPENSES	MONTHLY AVERAGE	ANNUAL AMOUNT	ANNUAL TOTAL
INSURANCE PREMIUMS (FIXED)			
Life	_____	_____	
Disability	_____	_____	
Medical	_____	_____	
Property and liability	_____	_____	
Auto	_____	_____	
Other	_____	_____	
			_____
TRANSPORTATION (FLEXIBLE)			
Car			
Gas/oil	_____	_____	
Repairs/maintenance	_____	_____	
Rental/loan/lease payments	_____	_____	
Garage/parking/tolls	_____	_____	
Public transportation/taxis	_____	_____	
			_____
PERSONAL (FLEXIBLE)			
Clothing	_____	_____	
Cleaning/laundry/shoe repair	_____	_____	
Beauty shop	_____	_____	
Toiletries/cosmetics	_____	_____	
Gifts	_____	_____	
Contributions	_____	_____	
Pet expenses	_____	_____	
			_____
MEDICAL (FLEXIBLE)			
Doctors/therapist	_____	_____	
Dentist	_____	_____	
Medication/eyeglasses	_____	_____	
			_____
EDUCATION (FLEXIBLE)			
Tuition	_____	_____	
Books/supplies/other	_____	_____	
Children's activities (camp, lessons, allowances, etc.)	_____	_____	
			_____
(2) **ENTERTAINMENT (FLEXIBLE)**			
Vacations/weekends away	_____	_____	
Movies/theater/VCR rentals	_____	_____	

EXPENSES	MONTHLY AVERAGE	ANNUAL AMOUNT	ANNUAL TOTAL
ENTERTAINMENT (CONTINUED)			
Books/magazines/newspapers	_____	_____	
Health club/dues	_____	_____	
Sports/hobbies	_____	_____	
Dining out	_____	_____	
Parties	_____	_____	
Wine/liquor	_____	_____	
Baby/pet/house sitters	_____	_____	
Other	_____	_____	
			_____
TAXES (FIXED)			
Federal	_____	_____	
State/city	_____	_____	
Other (unincorporated business tax, etc.)	_____	_____	
Social Security	_____	_____	
			_____
OTHER (FIXED)			
Alimony/child support	_____	_____	
Child care	_____	_____	
Business expense	_____	_____	
Education loans	_____	_____	
Home improvement loans	_____	_____	
Personal loans	_____	_____	
Other (credit cards, etc.)	_____	_____	
			_____
OTHER (FLEXIBLE)			
Durable purchases (car, boat, etc.)	_____	_____	
Fees (tax, legal, financial, etc.)	_____	_____	
			_____
CAPITAL EXPENDITURES (FLEXIBLE)			
401(k)/retirement plan	_____	_____	
IRA/Keogh/SEP	_____	_____	
Real estate investment	_____	_____	
Other investments	_____	_____	
			_____

(3)

TOTAL INCOME $_____

TOTAL FIXED EXPENSES $_____

TOTAL FLEXIBLE EXPENSES $_____

NET YEAR END CASH
(SHORTFALL) $_____

LESSON 8

CASH FLOW REVISITED

TERRY: I almost didn't come to this class. I didn't want all of you to see the wasteful ways I spend my money. I'm kind of embarrassed by it.

SUSAN: But I'll bet you're spending a lot of the money on things for your kids. I spend it totally on myself, and still can't account for thousands of dollars.

ANN: I'm glad you *all* showed up. It's an eye-opening experience to look at your cash flow, but we don't want to make ourselves feel guilty. We're going through an educational process, and one of the things we need to learn is that when you take control of how you spend your money you make decisions about how to live your life. You take control because *you* make the choices.

Let's talk about some of these "embarrassing" expenses. We all have them, and quite honestly, they are the easiest to correct because they are so obvious. I'll start.

My husband says I am the world's greatest gift-giver. In a way, he's right. It gives me great pleasure to buy a gift when I know it suits the person, and I don't like to wait for a special occasion. When I went through this exercise the first time, many years ago, I was shocked at how much I had spent on gifts in the previous year. I knew something had to be done! Coincidentally, this same year almost all of my friends were having babies. I had more than 20 baby gifts to buy, and I needed to come up with something clever and inexpensive. I went to a discount yarn store, bought a huge amount of blue and pink wool, and started knitting baby sweaters while I watched TV. Average cost: $4 per sweater, and everyone adored getting a homemade present.

You can't knit? Think of something you *can* do. It will make your gift unique and save a lot of money at the same time.

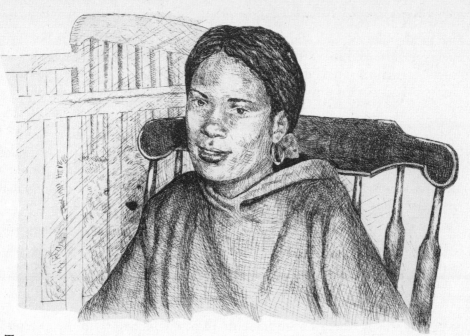

TERRY

STACY: My cousin had a baby, and I had no money to buy a gift. So I gave her a gift certificate for my baby-sitting services for ten hours. She told me it was the best gift she got.

TERRY: That was a great gift, Stacy. Actually, as you can see from my Cash Flow Worksheet, gift buying is a problem of mine. Especially at Christmas. Last year, we spent almost $2,000 during the holidays because we have so many relatives.

JANE: Our family came up with an idea that works great at Christmas. We have a lottery. Everyone picks a name out of a hat and is responsible for a gift for that one person. We make a range of how much to spend that is somewhat generous, so everyone gets one nice gift instead of a lot of not-so-nice gifts that you usually want to return. We buy a small toy for each of the children, and anyone who wants buys a savings bond for the parents to put away for the children's education. The whole family is happy.

CAROL: Jane, that is a wonderful idea! You all have such insight, maybe someone can help me with my problem area. Since my divorce I feel so guilty about my girls' not having the things I could give them when I was married that I buy whatever they ask for, put it on my charge card, and figure I'll worry about it later. I'm spending so much on finance charges and I'm getting deeper and deeper in debt.

STACY: I'm certainly no authority, but my best friend's parents got divorced, and her mother did the same thing. My friend got sort of messed up by it, because they never really talked about the situation, they just went shopping whenever they felt sad. My friend wanted her mother to be honest with her. She needed to share the feelings and work it through together. It took years, but they finally did.

SUSAN: Look, my parents are divorced and I'm still working it through. But I think Stacy makes a good point. Kids are a lot more resilient than we think. They are a part of the family for better or worse, and if they all chip in to solve a problem, they feel a part of the solution. I personally think children should work for the nonessential things they want. It seems to me a lot of us are ignorant about money because we were protected from it when we were young.

ANN: This is one of the reasons money holds such a mystique for many people. We need to recognize it for what it is and not expect it to make us happier, smarter, or more socially "in." Here is yet another reason that we need to create our *own* agenda of what is important—nobody can do this for you. *Only you.*
   Any questions about the entertainment section of expenses?

STACY: This is where I spend almost all of my money, with the exception of clothes and personal expenses. I know I'm eating dinner out way too much, but with working all day, it's the only time I can see my friends. Maybe I should learn to cook. I see about two movies a week, and go out with my friends every weekend. I think I'm going to have to set a limit on how much I spend a week on this.

ANN: OK. You're young and entertainment is important, but maybe you can make certain modifications that won't cramp your style too much. Instead of going out to the movies all the time, sometimes rent movies with friends; it costs a fraction of the movie ticket price, especially if you all chip in together. And learning to cook is a marvelous idea. You can buy the most expensive food for much less than what you would pay for meals in a restaurant, and you may find that you have master chef potential! Be careful to modify behavior, not totally cut out indulgences. You'll get frustrated and lose your desire to stay in control.

SUSAN: Other than my indulgences, the other place my money disappears is to taxes. I always knew I was paying a lot of taxes, but seeing them all together like this was a horror show!

ANN: True, it is upsetting to see how hard we work, and how much of the money goes to taxes, but there are some ways to improve the situation. First, for those of you who prepare your own tax returns, you must keep on top of the situation *all year,* not just on April 14. Have files organized for income and expense items. Be aware of the tax consequences of the financial decisions you make—it is never wise to make a decision solely based on the tax implication, but it certainly should be one factor in considering your options. If you employ an accountant, working in partnership with her is critical when doing your tax return. This means that you pay attention to the deductions to which you are entitled and not expect her to come up with creative solutions to your burden. For example, currently, you must spend at least $7\frac{1}{2}$ percent of your adjusted gross income on medical expenses before you can take a deduction. Let's say you're close to the threshold, but just a little short. It would be wise to get a physical, buy a pair of glasses, or so on *this year,* so that you can group your expenses and take a deduction. If you wait to do these things next year, you probably will not qualify in either year. Your accountant is not going to know you're close to the threshold until after the tax year is over and it's too late to get the deduction.

Employee benefits is another area to look at. Are you participating in your firm's 401(k) or profit-sharing plan? The money you contribute comes off your W-2 income and accumulates on a tax-deferred basis. (See the table on p. 16, which illustrates how much more money you accumulate in a tax-deferred account than in a taxable account.) Are you using your flexible spending account? This is a fund set aside at many companies for out-of-pocket health-care costs, child care, and/or elder care that allows you to spend pretax dollars on these items. What this means is that if you're in the 28 percent tax bracket, you will save 28 percent of the cost of child care, for example, if you pay the bills through this account. You must be careful only to put the amount of money you think you spend on these areas in the account, for if you don't spend all the money in the account within the year, it cannot be carried over into the next year; you lose it.

SUSAN: I think there's a flexible spending account where I work. I never did anything with it, because I wasn't sure there was a benefit. Are you saying that I could contribute money to an account held by my company, they will not deduct any taxes from this money, and I can pay my out-of-pocket medical bills from this account?

ANN: That's right. There's a limit to the amount you can put in the account (check with your employer), and as I said, you never want to put in more than you spend in one year because you cannot recover it if you do not use it for its intended purpose.

It's very obvious that no one cares to mention the clothing expense.

SUSAN: What is there to say? It's no surprise that *this* was a trouble spot.

STACY: But what can you do about it? You have to buy clothes!

JANE: Some of my friends introduced me to thrift shop buying, and I just love it.

The clothes are recycled from previous owners, but they are all in great condition, and they cost a fraction of what they would be new.

TERRY: I've gone to thrift shops, and they are fun. But mainly I go to the discount department stores and clearance centers. It's time-consuming, but if you're a patient shopper, you can find brand names at discount prices. An arrangement I have with my sister and my best friend may also be possible for some people. We all wear the same size. Every season, we each buy one dressy dress. Then when we have an affair to go to, we have three dresses to choose from.

CAROL: I'm going to have to find some friends that are my size, or go on a diet!

ANN: I must say, those are very creative alternatives. One key factor in buying clothes is to work with what you already have and try to buy accessories that will create new outfits; other tips include buying coordinated pieces that you can mix and match, and purchasing classic styles at the end of the season. I am sure you can all find ways to lessen what you spend on clothes. Find what works *for you* and be proud of yourself. Look at it this way, *anybody* can go into a store and pay retail. Only a person with desire and talent can get bargains!

Now, let's identify the areas of expenses we each need to work on. Make a notation on each category you want to target. In the next session when we discuss budgets, we'll concentrate on bringing these expenditures, in particular, under control.

Terry, will you share with us the areas you have identified to target?

TERRY: Sure. First, I need to balance my budget by cutting out $1,590 of expenses. Here are the places I think I can do it:

		FROM	TO	DIFFERENCE
1.	Clothing	$4,000	$3,500	$ 500
2.	Gifts	2,500	1,500	1,000
3.	Medical (flex. sp. acct.)	1,270	1,020	250
4.	Children's activities	2,050	1,550	500
5.	Vacations	2,500	2,000	500
6.	Baby sitters	600	480	120
				$2,870

ANN: That's great, Terry! Not only did you eliminate your $1,590 deficit, but you have an additional $1,280 to put toward your funding accounts.

You deserve a rest after doing such good work. Take some time off before beginning the next chapter.

BUDGET

■■■ ■ ■

ANN: Just mentioning budgeting makes most people shudder. It conjures up thoughts of keeping track of pennies and piles of paperwork. I hope we can change this image by making the process simple. First, as in previous lessons, we will *never* deal with pennies; please round all your numbers up to the next dollar. It cuts downs on the adding, and probably makes up for some of the items you will forget to put down. Second, we're not going to become obsessed with perfection. The object here is to allocate your funds in the best way possible for your priorities, not to have a perfectly balanced budget. And finally, remember the ultimate goal: to come up with the amount of money you require to afford your dreams.

Therefore, there should be a prominent section or sections of your budget to provide for your goals, whether it is your emergency fund, an education fund, a retirement fund, etc.

As we have done previously, let's take a quick look at the forms, run through the steps, and then we can discuss how to proceed.

Net Income Worksheet

		WEEK 1	WEEK 2	WEEK 3	WEEK 4	TOTALS
GROSS INCOME	SALARY					
	BONUS					
	INTEREST/DIVIDENDS					
	RENTAL INCOME					
	ALIMONY/CHILD SUPPORT					
	SOCIAL SECURITY					
	PENSION INCOME					
	UNEMPLOYMENT/DISABILITY					
	OTHER					
	OTHER					
	TOTAL GROSS MONTHLY INCOME					
DEDUCTIONS	FEDERAL TAX					
	STATE TAX					
	LOCAL TAX					
	SOCIAL SECURITY					
	ESTIMATED TAX PAYMENTS					
	OTHER					
	TOTAL MONTHLY DEDUCTIONS					
INCOME	INCOME − DEDUCTIONS = NET INCOME					

Fixed Expenses

NET MONTHLY INCOME _____

	YEARLY ESTIMATE	FIXED EXPENSES	JAN.	FEB.	MAR.	APR.	MAY	JUNE	JULY	AUG.	SEPT.	OCT.	NOV.	DEC.	TOTAL
HOME		Mortgage													
		Maint./rent													
		Real estate tax													
		Utilities													
		Telephone													
		Other													
INSURANCE		Medical													
		Disability													
		Auto													
		Prop./casualty													
		Life													
		Other													
DEBT		Auto loan													
		Education loan													
		Personal loan													
		Credit cards													
FUNDING		Emergency													
		Goal 1 (Ret./401[k]/ IRA/Keogh)													
		Goal 2													
		Goal 3													
TOTALS		Total fixed expenses													

TOTAL YEARLY FIXED EXPENSES	
AVERAGE MONTHLY FIXED EXPENSES	

Flexible Expenses—Monthly Log

	YEARLY ESTIMATE	FLEXIBLE EXPENSES	JAN.	FEB.	MAR.	APR.	MAY	JUNE	JULY	AUG.	SEPT.	OCT.	NOV.	DEC.	TOTAL
FOOD		Groceries/cleaning supplies													
		Lunches/snacks													
TRANS.		Car—gas/oil/repairs													
		Commutation (public trans.)													
		Other													
PERSONAL		Clothing													
		Cleaning/laundry													
		Beauty shop													
		Toiletries													
		Gifts													
		Contributions													
		Pets													
		Other													
ENTERTAINMENT		Vacations													
		Movies/theater/VCR													
		Bks./mags./newsp.													
		Sports/hobbies													
		Dining out													
		Parties													
		Baby/pet/house sitters													
		Other													
HOUSING		Maint./repairs													
		Help													
		Furnishings													
		Other													
EDUCATION		Tuition													
		Books/supplies													
		Lessons/camp													
		Allowances													
		Other													
MEDICAL (nonreimb.)		Doctors/therapists													
		Dentist													
		Medication													
		Eyeglasses													
		Other													
TOTAL		Total flexible expenses													

TOTAL YEARLY FLEXIBLE EXPENSES	
AVERAGE MONTHLY FLEXIBLE EXPENSES	

Flexible Expenses—Daily Log*

MONTH _____

	1	2	3	4	5	6	7	8	9	10	11	12	13	14	15	16	17	18	19	20	21	22	23	24	25	26	27	28	29	30	31	TOTAL
FOOD Groceries																																
Lunches/snacks																																
TRANS. Gas/oil/repairs																																
Commutation																																
Other																																
PERSONAL Clothing																																
Cleaning																																
Beauty shop																																
Toiletries																																
Gifts																																
Pets																																
Other																																
ENTERTAINMENT Movies/theater																																
Bks./mags./newsp.																																
Sports/hobbies																																
Dining out																																
Sitters																																
Other																																
HOUSING Maint./repairs																																
Help																																
Furnishings																																
Other																																
EDUC. Books																																
Lessons																																
Other																																
MISC.																																
																																TOTAL

*Make enlarged copies for personal use if you need to.

STEP 1: SOURCES OF INCOME

You already have this information from your cash flow statements. The only other step will be to subtract your tax deductions, estimated tax payments, and payroll deductions in order to arrive at a net income figure. Why is this number important? Simple—it's the amount you have to spend. You can find the deduction information on your most recent pay stub, or your last W-2 form. If you're self-employed, you will have to determine your net income figure by analyzing your estimated tax payments and your business deductions. (Consult with your accountant for help.) Use the Net Income Worksheet on p. 62.

Put this net income figure on top of the Fixed Expenses worksheet so you will be aware of how much you have to spend for your fixed *and* flexible expenses.

STEP 2: FIXED EXPENSES

Take the numbers from your Cash Flow Worksheet that constituted your fixed expenses and transfer them onto the Fixed Expenses budget sheet. Since these expenses do not change too much, you should be able to fill in this entire sheet. Be aware that some payments are not made every month (such as car insurance or in some cases, property tax). Record the payment in the month in which it occurs, for example, a $400 car insurance payment in January and July.

Once you have filled in the entire sheet, total all the columns, horizontally and vertically, and then add the total column. What you'll have is the sum of all your fixed expenses for the year. I know it's unbelievable, but don't flip out just yet. Take that number and divide it by 12, and this will give you your average monthly fixed expenses.

Many people like to keep a separate checking account for their fixed expenses. Each month, they are sure to deposit the number they came up with for the average monthly figure. This way, when the insurance bill is due, the money is in the account, and it's not necessary to scrounge around to come up with it. Others keep the money in a money-market account to earn better interest and transfer the fixed expense amount needed into their checking account each month.

I'll give one more plug for making specific categories on your Fixed Expenses list for each of your priority goals. Having these expenses anywhere but on your Fixed Expenses list is *not* an option. I want to emphasize this as forcefully as I can because it will be critical to your success. Pay for these goals as if they were another bill that can't be put off. Once you make this a habit, you'll be on your way to creating wealth. If you don't have the discipline to write a check from your account and deposit it into an investment account, arrange to have it automatically deducted at the bank and transferred to the account of your choice. Some people literally make themselves a bill and put it in the pile with their other fixed expenses.

How do you determine how much to put into this account? Well, as we discussed previously, 10 percent of your income would be nice, but if that's impossible, start with 5 percent, or 3 percent. It doesn't matter, just *start*. You'll increase the percentage as you get pay raises or bonuses.

STEP 3: FLEXIBLE EXPENSES

Here comes the hard part. Since flexible expenses don't happen on a regular basis, they're harder to track. You do have some idea now, as a result of filling in your Cash Flow Worksheets. Place the number you estimated on those sheets in the margin on the left of the Flexible Expenses sheet. Then, monthly, using your checkbook, credit card statements, and cash diary, fill in the actual amount spent in each of the categories. This is the only way you'll be truly sure of your accuracy. Add up each month's column to arrive at the total flexible expenses. Add this number to your fixed expenses number. If the amount is more than your income, you have some cutting to do. And, of course, the cutting is going to be from the flexible expenses.

STEP 4: DAILY LOG

For those of you who are having trouble keeping track of your daily expenses, you may find this day-to-day record handy. Each day is numbered, and major categories of expenses are designated. Take the figures from the small log you keep with you (or make a version of this one to carry) and plug in the numbers. You'll quickly be able to see at the end of the month where much of your cash is going.

Reader, work out your Fixed Expenses sheet (p. 63), and fill in as much as you can of the flexible sheets (pp. 64–65). You can see how Terry filled in hers on pp. 69–71, and note how she used her cash flow statement and her adjustments from p. 60 to come up with her budget figures. Then take a look at Terry's daily log (p. 71), which she has completed for March.

Net Income Worksheet

TERRY

		WEEK 1	WEEK 2	WEEK 3	WEEK 4	TOTALS
GROSS INCOME	SALARY	923	923	923	923	3692
	BONUS					
	INTEREST/DIVIDENDS					
	RENTAL INCOME					
	ALIMONY/CHILD SUPPORT					
	SOCIAL SECURITY					
	PENSION INCOME					
	UNEMPLOYMENT/DISABILITY					
	OTHER					
	OTHER					
	TOTAL GROSS MONTHLY INCOME					
DEDUCTIONS	FEDERAL TAX	83	83	83	83	332
	STATE TAX	29	29	29	29	116
	LOCAL TAX					
	SOCIAL SECURITY	71	71	71	71	284
	ESTIMATED TAX PAYMENTS					
	OTHER					
	TOTAL MONTHLY DEDUCTIONS					732
INCOME						
	INCOME − DEDUCTIONS = NET INCOME					2960

Fixed Expenses

TERRY

NET MONTHLY INCOME __2960__

	YEARLY ESTIMATE	FIXED EXPENSES	JAN.	FEB.	MAR.	APR.	MAY	JUNE	JULY	AUG.	SEPT.	OCT.	NOV.	DEC.	TOTAL
HOME		Mortgage													
	6600	Maint./rent	550	550	550	550	550	550	550	550	550	550	550	550	6600
		Real estate tax													
	600	Utilities	50	50	50	50	50	50	50	50	50	50	50	50	600
	480	Telephone	40	40	40	40	40	40	40	40	40	40	40	40	480
		Other													
INSURANCE		Medical													
		Disability													
	1300	Auto						650					650		1300
	100	Prop./casualty					100								100
	620	Life	155			155			155			155			620
		Other													
DEBT		Auto loan													
		Education loan													
		Personal loan													
	100	Credit cards	25	25	25	25									100
FUNDING	600	Emergency	50	50	50	50	50	50	50	50	50	50	50	50	600
	300	Goal 1 (Ret./401[k]/ IRA/Keogh)	25	25	25	25	25	25	25	25	25	25	25	25	300
	300	Goal 2	25	25	25	25	25	25	25	25	25	25	25	25	300
		Goal 3													
TOTALS	11,000	Total fixed expenses	920	765	765	920	840	1,390	895	740	740	895	740	1,390	11,000

TOTAL YEARLY FIXED EXPENSES	11,000
AVERAGE MONTHLY FIXED EXPENSES	917

Flexible Expenses—Monthly Log

TERRY

	YEARLY ESTIMATE	FLEXIBLE EXPENSES	JAN.	FEB.	MAR.	APR.	MAY	JUNE	JULY	AUG.	SEPT.	OCT.	NOV.	DEC.	TOTAL
FOOD	5,200	Groceries/cleaning supplies	412	395	420										
	1,020	Lunches/snacks	60	74	68										
TRANS.	1,350	Car—gas/oil/repairs	40	55	122										
		Commutation (public trans.)													
	100	Other Tolls	8	6	6										
PERSONAL	3,500	Clothing			230										
	400	Cleaning/laundry	25	28	40										
	200	Beauty shop		20	15										
	300	Toiletries		32	21										
	1,500	Gifts		75	104										
	200	Contributions													
	150	Pets	20												
	150	Other Tax Prep.													
ENTERTAINMENT	2,000	Vacations													
	400	Movies/theater/VCR	30	15	30										
	220	Bks./mags./newsp.	18	18	18										
	300	Sports/hobbies		40											
	2,100	Dining out	126	198	135										
	900	Parties	100												
	480	Baby/pet/house sitters	40	30	35										
	700	Other Wine/liquor	25												
HOUSING	500	Maint./repairs													
		Help													
		Furnishings													
	240	Other Cable TV	20	20	20										
EDUCATION		Tuition													
	200	Books/supplies	40												
	850	Lessons/camp	30	40	40										
	500	Allowances	40	40	40										
		Other													
MEDICAL (nonreimb.)	650	Doctors/therapists													
	250	Dentist		80											
	120	Medication			18										
		Eyeglasses													
		Other													
TOTAL	24,480	Total flexible expenses	1,034	1,166	1,362										

TOTAL YEARLY FLEXIBLE EXPENSES

AVERAGE MONTHLY FLEXIBLE EXPENSES

Flexible Expenses—Daily Log

TERRY
MONTH *March*

	Category	1	2	3	4	5	6	7	8	9	10	11	12	13	14	15	16	17	18	19	20	21	22	23	24	25	26	27	28	29	30	31	TOTAL
FOOD	Groceries		12		76			17			87		18			16					82				23				74		15		420
	Lunches/snacks			5	2	5	5		4			6	4			5	4	4	5				2	5	3		5		4				68
TRANS.	Gas/oil/repairs		12					15					12					15				12				15				41			122
	Commutation *Tolls*							1						1					1		1				1			1					6
	Other																																
PERSONAL	Clothing										65									145						20							230
	Cleaning					10																	22						8				40
	Beauty shop													15																			15
	Toiletries				16														5														21
	Gifts								50							12							12					30					104
	Pets																																
	Other																																
ENTERTAINMENT	Movies/theater							20													10												30
	Bks./mags./newsp.								5							4							5					4					18
	Sports/hobbies																																
	Dining out					38												42									55						135
	Sitters							10												10								15					35
	Other *Liquor*																																
HOUSING	Maint./repairs																																
	Help																																
	Furnishings																																
	Other																																
EDUC.	Books																																
	Lessons						10								10						10								10				40
	Other																																
MISC.																																	

TOTAL 1284

LESSON 10

■■ ■■ ■ ■ ■ ■■ ■ ■ ■ ■ ■ ■ ■■ ■ ■ ■ ■ ■ ■ ■ ■ ■ ■ ■■ ■ ■ ■ ■■

THE RETURN
OF THE BUDGET

■■ ■ ■■

ANN: Since no one sent me any hate mail this week, I assume you all survived filling out your budgets.

CAROL: Survived, yes, but with quite a few battle scars. One thing made me crazy! My fixed expenses are manageable only if I don't include paying off my debt. I can't see how I will ever have money for anything until I work this off.

ANN: There are different types of debt. Some debt builds assets, like the mortgage on a home, and offers tax benefits as well. But I get the feeling, Carol, that you are *not* talking about this type of debt but the kind used as an extension of income.

CAROL: You're right. It's mainly my credit cards. I feel out of control and frustrated by my inability to make any headway.

ANN: I know. It's frustrating to continue to pay for items you have already thrown out or forgotten about. That is why we want to learn how to use credit cards correctly. Carol, your *first* project *is* to get rid of your credit card debt, and there will be a lesson with worksheets to help you later in this book. Once you have accomplished this (and *you will*, I promise), think of all the money you'll have available for the items you *really* want.

CAROL: I'll feel like a huge weight has been lifted from my shoulders.

TERRY: I don't know if I'm spending too much in some areas. Is there a certain percentage of income we should be spending on each category?

JANE: I read somewhere that you shouldn't spend more than 25 percent or 30 percent of your income on housing and 10 percent on debt repayment.

STACY: Doesn't it really depend on each person? I don't make that much money, but I also don't have any kids to spend it on.

ANN: Good point, Stacy. It does depend on your particular situation. Guidelines are based on the "average" person, whoever that is. If you have set your priorities, can cover your fixed expenses (including the amount set aside for your goals), and have your discretionary expenses under control, you've found the correct percentages for you. Locking ourselves into rigid patterns will only lead to frustration. We must recognize that as our needs change, so will our spending and saving strategies. We created the habits we have now; we can also change them to fit our needs.

SUSAN: Any suggestions on how to get the money from my paycheck into my investment account without my seeing it? It's so hard not to spend money I think I have sitting there.

STACY: Aren't there payroll deduction plans where it comes automatically out of your check and you don't see it?

ANN: Yes, and they're the perfect solution for Susan's problem (and almost everyone else's, I might add). Contact your employee benefits department and they will help you with the plans your company manages, which may include a 401(k) plan, a pension plan, a U.S. Savings Bond payroll deduction plan, etc. Here are some others you can set up on your own:

1. Automatic transfer from your checking account to a savings or money-market account. Set it up with your bank; there's usually no charge.
2. Automatic transfer from your checking account to a mutual fund. Set it up between your bank and mutual fund. Usually there is no fee, but there may be a minimum amount required for transfer.
3. Automatic transfer from your checking account to a brokerage account. Set it up between your bank and broker. Usually there is no fee or minimum.

STACY: I need to ask a question about the flexible expenses. You know, I want to have my own apartment. One of the categories was household maintenance. I realized I'm going to need so much stuff starting out. How will I ever be able to buy even the basic things a person needs?

CAROL: I can remember when I first got married. We had absolutely nothing. Our furniture was all donated from relatives, and every month, we bought one necessity, like a coffeepot or a vacuum. Many of the items we found at thrift shops.

SUSAN: I developed a group of friends where I lived when I was starting out. We shared the household appliances you don't need every day. For instance, I bought a rug cleaner, one of my friends bought a floor polisher, and the third bought a huge coffee maker. Not only did it save us money, but it also took up a lot less space.

TERRY: Gee, I thought we were so smart. We did the same thing in my neighborhood with lawn equipment. We all chipped in and bought a lawn mower, a leaf blower, a hedge clipper, and a snow blower. They're housed in a shed, and we have a schedule for usage. We have a fund for maintenance, and so far, it has worked great.

JANE: My friends and I have taken this one step further. We formed a group for sharing services. We all wrote down what we could contribute to the group, and we barter among ourselves. I don't work on Fridays, so I could contribute time. I've run errands, baby-sat, or carpooled. In return, I've had my taxes done, my hair cut, and curtains made for my bedroom.

CAROL: That is so clever! I'm going to organize a group like that in my town. It's perfect for people who can't work full-time, or maybe want a part-time job, but want to utilize their talents.

ANN: What a great group of women you are! I learn as much from you as you do from me, which is so exciting for me. By pooling our experiences, we open ourselves to our unlimited potential.

    Stacy, did you get any ideas you can use?

STACY: Well, I would have preferred that someone just volunteer to furnish my apartment for me, and then I wouldn't have to struggle to get what I need. But I'm starting to understand that it isn't going to happen that way.

ANN: You'll be better off in the long run. The best way to build self-esteem is to earn what you have. When someone just "gives" it to you, there is so much less appreciation of its value. It's unrealistic to "have it all" right now. Plan, work, achieve—it's the way to get what you want. And the bonus is that you're not dependent on anyone.

    Were there any other areas you discovered where you spent a lot more than you estimated?

SUSAN: When I totaled up what I spent on books and magazines last year, I was floored. It doesn't seem like much when I'm doing it, but it certainly did add up.

ANN: You could get a library card and then take out books and read magazines for free. But if you enjoy the convenience of having them at home, or have trouble getting the book back on time, you might set up your own lending library. For years, I've been sharing magazines with a number of friends. We each get a subscription to one and then pass them around. We do the same thing with books. If I read a good one, it makes the rounds to all my friends.

TERRY: The one area of expenses I hate to cut out is activities for my children. Even though it's expensive, I feel it's very important.

ANN: Fine, you have made this a priority, and that is perfectly acceptable. Let's try to think of ways to help Terry fund her children's lessons and recreation. Any ideas?

STACY: How about the barter idea. Piano lessons for some service Terry can do.

JANE: Or how about telling relatives that instead of fancy toys for birthdays, your daughter would love ballet lessons. If that's too expensive, how about ballet slippers or a tutu? Not only would it save you the cost, but it would give Grandma an interest in her grandchild's development.

CAROL: Maybe by shopping around you can find a place to get the same lesson for less money. Like a part-time person wanting to teach clarinet, or a student.

ANN: You guys don't even need me here anymore. As Professor Higgins said, "I think you've got it!"

Continue to work with your budgets. Take the ideas we've discussed today and open yourself up to the alternatives available to you. By redefining priorities and changing spending habits you're going to "find" the money you need to finance your goals.

Next week we'll determine how much money is needed for a particular goal. It will give you a better idea how much you need to allocate from your income each paycheck.

▪▬▪ ▪▬▪ ▬▪▬ ▪▬▪ ▪▬▪ ▬▪▬ ▪▬▪ ▪▬▪ ▬▪▬ ▪▬▪ ▪▬▪

HOW MUCH SHOULD YOU BE INVESTING IN YOUR GOALS?

▬▪▬ ▪▬▪

ANN: We've spoken a few times about putting 10 percent of earnings into an account to finance your goals. For many people with long-term projects this will work just fine. However, you may want to know how much money you need to put away each week for a specific goal, especially if you have a time constraint. For example, if you have six years until your child goes to college and you don't wish to postpone enrollment, you'll want to make sure you are accumulating enough money to have the tuition when you need it.

Let's take one of your goals and illustrate how you can work out the payments for yourself. Who would like to volunteer one of her goals to use as an example?

SUSAN: I would. Can we use my goal for a down payment on a summer house?

ANN: Sure. Let's go through the steps of the Goal Planning Worksheet (p. 79) using Susan's down payment. Then each of you can work on your own goals. You may have one priority like Carol's credit cards, which you want to pay off before you start on any others. Or you may want to work on a few projects at once.

STEP 1

The first step is *defining the goal*—in this case a down payment on a house. OK, Susan, how much do you need and what's your timetable for getting it?

SUSAN: Well, houses in the town in which I've been renting average around $200,000. I think I should have at least 20 percent down—let's make it $50,000 so I have money for closing costs and some decorating. I would like to have it for my forty-fifth birthday—that's in three years.

Susan

Ann: Fine. Your target date is in three years (we'll put this on line 2 of the chart) and the amount needed, $50,000, on line 3.

STEP 2

Now, Susan, how much have you already saved toward your down payment?

Susan: Only about $5,700.

Ann: That's fine. Put $5,700 on line 4. How do you have it invested?

Susan: It's in a bond mutual fund earning 6 percent.

Ann: OK. If you continue to earn 6 percent on this $5,700 for the next three years, you will obviously have more than $5,700 at the end of that time. To figure

Goal Planning Worksheet

STEP 1   1. Define goal   _____

               2. Year you need funds   _____

               3. Total amount needed   _____

STEP 2   4. Amount you have already saved   _____

               5. Amount this will be when you need funds (see Future Value Table)   _____

               6. Remaining amount not covered by current savings   _____

STEP 3   7. Amount of total expenses that may be met by outside sources (gifts, loans, financial aid, etc.)   _____

               8. Net amount not covered by current savings or outside sources   _____

STEP 4   9. Amount you would have to put away each year to reach goal (see Annuity Factors Table)   _____

             10. Amount you should invest each month   _____

             11. Amount you should invest each week   _____

Goal Planning Worksheet   Susan

STEP 1	1. Define goal	*Summer House*
	2. Year you need funds	*In 3 years*
	3. Total amount needed	*50,000*
STEP 2	4. Amount you have already saved	*5,700*
	5. Amount this will be when you need funds (see Future Value Table)	*6,789 (5,700 X 1.1910)*
	6. Remaining amount not covered by current savings	*43,211 (50,000 – 6,789)*
STEP 3	7. Amount of total expenses that may be met by outside sources (gifts, loans, financial aid, etc.)	*25,000*
	8. Net amount not covered by current savings or outside sources	*18,211 (43,211 – 25,000)*
STEP 4	9. Amount you would have to put away each year to reach goal (see Annuity Factors Table)	*5,720 (18,211 ÷ 3.1836)*
	10. Amount you should invest each month	*477 per month*
	11. Amount you should invest each week	*110 per week*

out how much you will actually have, refer to the Future Value Table (below). Notice across the top of the chart there are percentages. This is the amount of interest you are earning. Susan's mutual fund currently earns 6 percent, so we will focus on that column. The numbers in the column marked "period" stand for years. Susan has three years before she's using the money. Look at the factor at the intersection of 6 percent and three years—it's 1.1910. If you multiply $5,700 by

FUTURE VALUE TABLE

PERIOD	3%	4%	5%	6%	7%	8%	9%	10%
1	1.0300	1.0400	1.0500	1.0600	1.0700	1.0800	1.0900	1.1000
2	1.0609	1.0816	1.1025	1.1236	1.1449	1.1664	1.1881	1.2100
3	1.0927	1.1249	1.1576	1.1910	1.2250	1.2597	1.2950	1.3310
4	1.1255	1.1699	1.2155	1.2625	1.3108	1.3605	1.4116	1.4641
5	1.1593	1.2657	1.2763	1.3382	1.4026	1.4693	1.5386	1.6105
6	1.1941	1.2653	1.3401	1.4185	1.5007	1.5869	1.6771	1.7716
7	1.2299	1.3159	1.4071	1.5036	1.6058	1.7138	1.8280	1.9487
8	1.2668	1.3686	1.4775	1.5938	1.7182	1.8509	1.9926	2.1436
9	1.3048	1.4233	1.5513	1.6895	1.8385	1.9990	2.1719	2.3579
10	1.3439	1.4802	1.6289	1.7908	1.9672	2.1589	2.3674	2.5937
11	1.3842	1.5395	1.7103	1.8983	2.1049	2.3316	2.5804	2.8531
12	1.4258	1.6010	1.7959	2.0122	2.2522	2.5182	2.8127	3.1384
13	1.4685	1.6651	1.8856	2.1329	2.4098	2.7196	3.0658	3.4523
14	1.5126	1.7317	1.9799	2.2609	2.5785	2.9372	3.3417	3.7975
15	1.5580	1.8009	2.0789	2.3966	2.7590	3.1722	3.6425	4.1772
16	1.6047	1.8730	2.1829	2.5404	2.9522	3.4259	3.9703	4.5950
17	1.6528	1.9479	2.2920	2.6928	3.1588	3.7000	4.3275	5.0545
18	1.7024	2.0258	2.4066	2.8543	3.3799	3.9960	4.7171	5.5599
19	1.7535	2.1068	2.5270	3.0256	3.6165	4.3157	5.1417	6.1159
20	1.8061	2.1911	2.6533	3.2071	3.8697	4.6610	5.6044	6.7275
21	1.8603	2.2788	2.7860	3.3996	4.1406	5.0338	6.1088	7.4002
22	1.9161	2.3699	2.9253	3.6035	4.4304	5.4365	6.6586	8.1403
23	1.9736	2.4647	3.0715	3.8197	4.7405	5.8715	7.2579	8.9543
24	2.0328	2.5633	3.2251	4.0489	5.0724	6.3412	7.9111	9.8497
25	2.0938	2.6658	3.3864	4.2919	5.4274	6.8485	8.6231	10.834
26	2.1566	2.7725	3.5557	4.5494	5.8074	7.3964	9.3992	11.918
27	2.2213	2.8834	3.7335	4.8223	6.2139	7.9881	10.245	13.110
28	2.2879	2.9987	3.9201	5.1117	6.6488	8.6271	11.167	14.421
29	2.3566	3.1187	4.1161	5.4184	7.1143	9.3173	12.172	15.863
30	2.4273	3.2434	4.3219	5.7435	7.6123	10.062	13.267	17.449

1.1910, it will tell you how much money you'll have at the end of the three-year period: $6,789. This is the amount you put in the blank next to line 5.

The amount remaining that is not covered by current savings would be $50,000 minus $6,789, which equals $43,211 (see line 6).

STEP 3

Susan, are there any sources you have that could help you assemble the remaining amount? Things like gifts, loans from relatives, loans from plans at work?

SUSAN: I certainly can't depend on any gifts or loans from relatives, but I could borrow from my plan at work. I wouldn't want to borrow more than $25,000.

ANN: OK. Put $25,000 on line 7. Let me just point out that borrowing from your 401(k) plan is an option as long as you are aware of the consequences: You have a certain time period in which to pay the money back (with interest); you cannot borrow again from the fund until the money is totally paid up; and if you should leave your job (or get fired) you must pay the money in full or you will pay tax and a penalty on the outstanding amount. Then line 8 becomes $43,211 minus $25,000, which equals $18,211. This is the net amount not covered by current savings or outside sources.

STEP 4

I have provided another table, which is titled Annuity Factors Table (p. 82). Let's assume you can earn the same 6 percent interest. Find the factor that corresponds to 6 percent, and under the number of periods, find 3 for three years. As you can see, the number where these values intersect is 3.1836.

Divide the amount you need, $18,211, by 3.1836. The answer is $5,720, which means each year for the next three years you would need to add to your down payment account that amount to reach your goal. Saving $5,720 per year is $477 per month or $110 per week.

Doesn't it sound much more manageable to come up with $110 per week than it does to come up with $50,000? I think so.

You can follow this format for whatever you are financing, whether it is a college education, starting a business, or anything. Once you have used the Future Value Table and the Annuity Factors Table a few times, they will pose no problem for you. If you get confused, go over our example with Susan's down payment.

ANNUITY FACTORS TABLE

Number of Periods	3%	4%	5%	6%	7%	8%	9%	10%
1	1.0000	1.0000	1.0000	1.0000	1.0000	1.0000	1.0000	1.0000
2	2.0300	2.0400	2.0500	2.0600	2.0700	2.0800	2.0900	2.1000
3	3.0909	3.1216	3.1525	3.1836	3.2149	3.2464	3.2781	3.3100
4	4.1836	4.2465	4.3101	4.3746	4.4399	4.5061	4.5731	4.6410
5	5.3091	5.4163	5.5256	5.6371	5.7507	5.8666	5.9847	6.1051
6	6.4684	6.6330	6.8019	6.9753	7.1533	7.3359	7.5233	7.7156
7	7.6625	7.8983	8.1420	8.3938	8.6540	8.9228	9.2004	9.4872
8	8.8923	9.2142	9.5491	9.8975	10.259	10.636	11.028	11.435
9	10.159	10.582	11.026	11.491	11.978	12.487	13.021	13.579
10	11.463	12.006	12.577	13.180	13.816	14.486	15.192	15.937
11	12.807	13.486	14.206	14.971	15.783	16.645	17.560	18.531
12	14.192	15.025	15.917	16.869	17.888	18.977	20.140	21.384
13	15.617	16.626	17.713	18.882	20.140	21.495	22.953	24.522
14	17.086	18.291	19.598	21.015	22.550	24.214	26.019	27.975
15	18.598	20.023	21.578	23.276	25.129	27.152	29.360	31.772
16	20.156	21.824	23.657	25.672	27.888	30.324	33.003	35.949
17	21.761	23.697	25.840	28.212	30.840	33.750	36.973	40.544
18	23.414	25.645	28.132	30.905	33.999	37.450	41.301	45.599
19	25.116	27.671	30.539	33.760	37.379	41.446	46.018	51.159
20	26.870	29.778	33.066	36.785	40.995	45.762	51.160	57.275
21	28.676	31.969	35.719	39.992	44.865	50.422	56.764	64.002
22	30.536	34.248	38.505	43.392	49.005	55.456	62.873	71.402
23	32.452	36.617	41.430	46.995	53.436	60.893	69.531	79.543
24	34.426	39.082	44.502	50.815	58.176	66.764	76.789	88.497
25	36.459	41.645	47.727	54.864	63.249	73.105	87.700	98.347
26	38.553	44.311	51.113	59.156	68.676	79.954	93.323	109.18
27	40.709	47.084	54.669	63.705	74.483	87.350	102.72	121.09
28	42.930	49.967	58.402	68.528	80.697	95.338	112.96	134.20
29	45.218	52.966	62.322	73.639	87.346	103.96	124.13	148.63
30	47.575	56.084	66.438	79.058	94.460	113.28	136.30	164.49

FINDING THE RIGHT INVESTMENTS

ANN: And now the moment you have all been waiting for. I'm going to tell you what investments to buy. Well, not exactly. I'm going to explain how to find the right investment for what it is you are funding, and then provide information about various investments that you'll be able to work with to determine on your own or with the help of a professional what the appropriate vehicle is for you.

Most people approach the task of buying investments totally backward. They buy a stock that a friend or relative has told them will double or triple and they never give a minute's thought to what that money is funding. They are thinking only about how much more money they will have over a short period of time. First, it rarely works out that way, and second, even if it does, they continue to repeat the process until a major loss is incurred that wipes out all the gains and many times puts them in the loss column.

Instead, let's continue with our approach:

1. Creating goals that are priorities for us and have such meaning that we are *excited* about finding ways to fund them.
2. Discovering how much we need for each goal and developing a plan.

The next logical step is

3. Finding an investment that is appropriate to the objective.

So, Susan, your goal is to have a down payment for your new home. What type of investment do you think would work here?

SUSAN: I have no idea. Something that will make a lot of money quickly because I need it within three years.

ANN: And what's more important? Protecting the amount you are saving or getting the highest return?

SUSAN: I guess protecting what I have. If I lose this money, it will take me years to replace it.

ANN: Exactly. That is why you cannot risk this money by investing it in something that will require a long-term commitment, such as the stock market. To buy stocks you need at least a four- to five-year time horizon because in any given period the market can rise or fall. You need to be able to withstand a major down-draft in prices and have the time necessary to participate in the recovery.

JANE: So what you are saying is that all money that you need to use within four to five years should be kept as safe as possible? This would also include an emergency fund, I assume. And what in the world is safe anyway?

ANN: Understanding that there is risk in *every* investment, we need to define the risk to see if it's all right in terms of our funding needs. For instance, there are some people who only feel safe if their money is hidden under the mattress. They trust no one. But even this carries some risks.

STACY: Yeah, you could get robbed. Or what about a fire?

ANN: True, these are risks attached to keeping the money under the mattress. But the real danger here is the purchasing power you'll lose by *not* investing the money. If you keep your funds uninvested for 20 years, when you do spend it, it will buy a lot less than it does today. So what has happened is the value of your dollar has decreased. The only way to keep up is to have the dollar grow by investing it and earning dividends, interest, or capital gains.

So we need to find places to invest this "safe" money where we could get our hands on it if there were an emergency, or if that perfect house came along. These would be the instruments we term "liquid": cash, checking account, savings account, money-market funds, Treasury bills, short-term CDs. We want our entire portfolio to be as diversified as possible, even in our liquid investments. Therefore, just having a checking account is not enough, because we want to earn the most we possibly can while maintaining our objective of liquidity. If the money is earmarked for an emergency fund, it's unlikely you'll need all of the proceeds the same day. You'll need it over a period of time. For that reason, a three-month or a six-month CD will give you a better interest rate than a savings account, but you will not be able to touch it until maturity without paying a penalty. By mixing the types of investments even within the defensive level, you get a better rate of return while protecting yourself against overexposure at any one institution.

SUSAN: You know, this business of looking for the appropriate investment reminds me of something that happened to a woman at work. She was getting married, and her family was giving her a big wedding. Two weeks before the wedding the stock market went down hundreds of points—I'm sure you remember the crash in 'eighty-seven. Anyway, her father lost so much money that day, he had to call all the people who were invited to the wedding to tell them they couldn't come because he didn't have the money to pay for the reception.

STACY: How horrible. What happened to the woman?

SUSAN: She got married anyway, but only the immediate family was there. I felt sorry for her father, though. What guilt he felt.

ANN: I bet he did. What an example of an inappropriate investment! Two weeks before a wedding, the money should be liquid, not in the stock market. Thank you, Susan. That was a story that truly illustrates the point.

TERRY: What about investments for goals that go beyond five years? I'm afraid to venture beyond the defensive type of investment. I don't want to lose my money under any circumstances; we work too hard for it.

CAROL: I agree. I'd rather make a lot less on my money and know it's safe than shoot for a huge gain and risk losing it.

ANN: You're not alone. Many women feel exactly as you do. For the long-term investments (those over 5 years), you may actually be losing money by keeping it in defensive investments because the rate of interest you receive will not keep up with the rate of inflation. If we review history, we'll see that over a 55-year period, bonds have returned on average 4.5 percent, while stocks have returned over 10 percent. We need to understand that there's a bigger risk in *not* investing in the stock market over the long term than there is in participating.

CAROL: But who knows what to buy in the stock market? It seems too complicated to get involved.

ANN: Actually, I agree that for most people, picking individual stocks is too complicated. This is why mutual funds were born. A mutual fund will give you a diversified portfolio and professional management with relatively low transaction costs.

JANE: But there are thousands of mutual funds selling all kinds of products. How do you decide which one is right for you?

ANN: Good question. Again, we go to our goals. If our aim is for a college education for our children, we will want to concentrate on a mutual fund that specializes in growth stocks (pays little if any dividends but concentrates on increasing the share price) until the child is four to five years away from enrollment. Then we switch back to our defensive strategy and move the money from the growth fund into an investment that will give us the best interest without the risk of losing the principal.

Using retirement as our example, if you have 25 years until you retire, you should be looking for a fund or funds that emphasize stocks. You may want to diversify into different types of stocks. For instance, maybe a blue-chip fund (large, well-established companies that pay dividends), a global fund (stocks from many countries), and an aggressive growth fund (smaller companies with potential to grow faster than the general economy).

STACY: Is there a way to learn about mutual funds? Like a course or something?

ANN: Yes, and I think this is a course worth taking. So many people who are disappointed in their mutual fund investments really had no idea when they bought them what they were buying into. It's very important to get the prospectus on the mutual fund you are interested in and read it.

JANE: Have you ever looked at that thing? It's printed on paper way below recycled quality and just appears to be a jumble of information.

ANN: I know, it looks very unappealing, but it can make the difference between success and failure. Once you know how to read one of them, you can read *all* of them; they basically follow the same format. What will reading a prospectus teach you? Among other things:

1. How much you are being charged to participate. Is it no-load (no upfront commission)? Are there redemption fees (charges to cash in)? Are there 12(b)1 fees (charges for advertising costs)? What are the annual fees (management fees charged every year for running the fund)? Do they charge a sales fee on reinvested dividends (dividends that you put into more shares instead of taking the money)? You need to compare *all* the fees to determine which is the most cost-effective for you.
2. What is the fund investing in? Stocks, bonds, a combination of stocks and bonds, options, etc.
3. What is the philosophy of the fund? Going for growth, high dividends, producing returns that mirror the Dow Jones Stock Averages, etc.
4. Who the fund managers are and a history of the investment company.

5. How the performance has been for the past 10 years or for the life of the fund.

You can't just put your money into any old fund and think you have done your job. The great thing about a mutual fund is that if you have done your investigation properly, and if you have diversified well among funds, you probably will not have to move the money very often to be effective.

Look for a course in your area that will teach you to read the prospectus. It is usually done in *one night*. Certainly not time consuming, considering the benefit you will derive from it. Most adult education programs at colleges and even some high schools have a class in mutual funds. You can also read about it. I have listed some worthwhile books and rating services in the back of this book to help you.

CAROL: I am unclear about all the investments you are discussing, from the liquid investments to the more long-term ones. It would help me to see them defined and to understand where they can be purchased and how much they should cost. Then I could match the investment to my goal.

ANN: Great idea. Let's take some time to break down the investments as Carol suggested.

[*See pp. 88–95.*]

INVESTMENT ALTERNATIVES
MT=Medium-term / LT=Long-term

Investment	Definition	Risk	Tax Consequences	Minimum Investment	Institutions Offering	Cost
Savings passbook	Bank interest. Rate varies with current interest rates.	FDIC insured up to $100,000. Liquid.	Interest taxed as ordinary income.	None	Banks	None
Bank money market	Interest higher than savings account. Diversified short-term bonds. Specific funds available; e.g., only U.S. govt. bonds.	FDIC insured up to $100,000. Liquid.	Interest taxed as ordinary income.	Varies. $500 to $2,500.	Banks	None
Money market	Interest varies depending on type of short-term investments in portfolio. Can be taxable, tax-free, govt., etc.	Varies according to type of holdings. Liquid.	If taxable holdings, ordinary income. If tax-exempt holdings, no tax (depending on where one lives).	Varies. $250 to $1,000.	Mutual funds	Usually no sales fee. Management fee each year up to 1%.
Certificates of deposit	Interest varies depending on length of maturity. Rate fixed from 30 days to 5 years or more.	FDIC insured up to $100,000 if at a bank or brokerage house. Liquid with penalty for early withdrawal.	Interest taxed as ordinary income.	Varies. Banks: $500 to $2,500, depending on term. Brokerage house: $1,000.	Banks, S&Ls / Brokerage house	No charge, penalty for early withdrawal. Nominal or no charge.

INVESTMENT ALTERNATIVES (cont.)
MT=Medium-term / LT=Long-term

Investment	Definition	Risk	Tax Consequences	Minimum Investment	Institutions Offering	Cost
U.S. savings bonds (Series EE)	Minimum interest of 4%, if held for 5 years. Rate can be higher. Do not receive cash interest; it accrues and receive upon redemption. Can redeem after 6 mos., or hold for 30 years.	Fully backed by U.S. govt. MT, LT	Exempt from state and city tax. Federally taxed when redeemed. If used for college tuition, may be fully or partially tax-exempt.	Minimum $25 for a $50 face value. Maximum per year $15,000.	Banks, thrifts, Federal Reserve Bank, payroll deduction plans. For current rate information: 800-487-2663.	No charge
U.S. savings bonds (Series HH)	Can exchange EE bonds after 6 months or at redemption. Receive cash interest. Maturity 10 years.	Fully backed by U.S. govt. MT, LT	Exempt from state and city tax. If swap from EE bonds, don't have to pay tax on EE interest until redeem HH bonds.	Minimum $500 redemption value.	Banks, thrifts, Federal Reserve Bank.	No charge
Treasury bills	A U.S. govt. obligation with the shortest term, 3 mos., 6 mos., 1 year. Pays no interest at regular intervals; instead, sold at discounted price, which is the difference between the interest earned and the	Backed by U.S. govt. Safest investment. However, if sold before matures, can lose principal if interest rates rise. Liquid.	Interest is exempt from state and local tax. Federally taxed as ordinary income.	$10,000, then in increments of $5,000.	Federal Reserve Bank, all branches. In person or through the mail. For an application, write to: Bureau of the Public Debt, Department of the Treasury, 1300 C St., S.W., Washington, DC 20239,	No fee, but need certified check for first subscription.

INVESTMENT ALTERNATIVES (*cont.*)
MT=Medium-term / LT=Long-term

INVESTMENT	DEFINITION	RISK	TAX CONSEQUENCES	MINIMUM INVESTMENT	INSTITUTIONS OFFERING	COST
Treasury bills (*cont.*)	face amount received at maturity.				or call the Federal Reserve nearest you.	
					Brokerage house: Subscribe with your broker in your existing account.	Transaction fee ranging from $25 to $75.
					Bank: Subscribe with your banker in a Treasury-bill account.	Transaction fee of $50.
Treasury notes	A U.S. govt. obligation with maturities of 2 to 10 years. Purchased at face value. Pays interest semiannually.	Same as Treasury bill. MT, LT	Same as Treasury bill.	For 2- and 4-year, note minimum is $5,000; all others, minimum is $1,000.	Same as Treasury bill.	Same as Treasury bill.
Treasury bonds	A U.S. govt. obligation with maturities of 10 years and up. Purchased at face value. Pays interest semiannually.	Same as Treasury bill. MT, LT	Same as Treasury bill.	Minimum $1,000.	Same as Treasury bill.	Same as Treasury bill.

INVESTMENT ALTERNATIVES (cont.)
MT=Medium-term / LT=Long-term

Investment	Definition	Risk	Tax Consequences	Minimum Investment	Institutions Offering	Cost
U.S. govt.-sponsored agency	An obligation of a subdivision of the U.S. govt. Most common are Export-Import Bank, Federal Housing Administration, and the U.S. Postal Service. Term varies from 9 mos. to 20 years, depending on type of bond. Interest payments vary from monthly to yearly.	Backed by U.S. govt. MT, LT	Interest is exempt from state and local taxes.	From $1,000 to $10,000	Brokerage house Mutual fund Banks	Minimum $50, then dependent on amt. of bonds; usually around 1% of value. Varies. Check load, mgmt. fee, other fees. Minimum $38; then dependent on amt. of bonds; usually around 1% of value.
Ginnie Mae bonds	Govt. National Mortgage Administration. Pool of individual mortgages. Pays monthly; part interest, part return of principal. At maturity, value of bond is zero. Maturities 1 to 25 years.	Backed by U.S. govt. Can be negatively affected by prepayment of underlying mortgages. MT, LT	Interest fully taxable. Return of capital not taxable.	Individual bond, $25,000, available in mutual fund or unit trust.	Brokerage house Mutual fund Banks	Minimum $50; then dependent on amt. of bonds; usually around 1% of value. Varies. Check load, mgmt. fee, redemption fee, other fees. Minimum $38; then dependent on amt. of bonds; usually around 1% of value.

Investment	Definition	Risk	Tax Consequences	Minimum Investment	Institutions Offering	Cost
Federal agency bonds	Various agencies, such as Fannie Mae, Sallie Mae, Federal Home Loan Bank, etc. Maturities and interest payments vary.	Backed by individual agency. Not U.S. govt. guaranteed. MT, LT	Interest exempt from state and local tax	From $1,000 to $5,000	Brokerage house	Minimum $50; then dependent on amt. of bonds; usually around 1% of value.
					Mutual fund	Varies. Check load, mgmt. fee, redemption fee, other fees.
					Banks	Minimum $38; then dependent on amt. of bonds; usually around 1% of value.
Municipal bonds	Debt obligations of state and local govts. Maturities in short-, medium-, and long-term bonds. Usually cannot be redeemed prematurely by municipality for 10 years.	Depends on issuer. For highest quality, buy those rated AAA or AA. If held until maturity, redeemed at par; if sold prior to maturity, interest rate and liquidity risk. MT, LT	Most bonds are federally tax-free. If purchased from municipality where you live, no state or city tax. All states exempt tax on bonds from Puerto Rico, Guam, and the Virgin Islands.	Usually $5,000	Brokerage house	Minimum $50; $5 to $10 per bond. Varies. Check load, mgmt. fee, redemption fee, other fees.
					Mutual fund	
					Banks	Minimum $38; then dependent on amt. of bond; usually 1% of value.
Corporate bonds	Debt obligation of a corporation. Maturities in short-, medium-,	Depends on issuer. For highest quality, buy those rated AAA or AA.	Fully taxable	$5,000	Brokerage house	Minimum $50; $5 to $10 per bond. Varies. Check load, mgmt. fee,
					Mutual fund	

INVESTMENT ALTERNATIVES (cont.)
MT=Medium-term / LT=Long-term

Investment	Definition	Risk	Tax Consequences	Minimum Investment	Institutions Offering	Cost
Corporate bonds (cont.)	and long-term bonds. Call protection from 5 to 10 years.	If coupon rate very high, may be "junk" bond. If held until maturity, redeemed at par; if sold prior to maturity, interest rate and liquidity risk. MT, LT			Banks	redemption fee, other fees. Minimum $38; $35 for first bond purchased, $4 for second through fifth, $3 for sixth through twentieth, and $2 thereafter.
Convertible bonds	Mix of stock and bond. Pays interest like a bond, and convertible into a fixed number of shares at a certain price.	Provides fixed income and opportunity to participate if stock appreciates. But can convert to stock only if price exceeds a certain level. LT	Interest fully taxable. No tax consequences at time of conversion into stock. Any gains fully taxable.	$1,000	Brokerage house Mutual fund Bank	Minimum $50; $5 to $15 commission per bond. Varies. Check load, mgmt. fee, redemption fee, other fees. Minimum $38; then dependent on number of bonds; usually 1% of value.
Zero coupon bonds	Debt obligation of federal govt., municipality, or corporation. Purchased at a discount from face value. Receive no interest until redemption.	If underlying issuer defaults, loss of all interest and principal (not a problem with zeros issued by U.S. govt.). LT	Even though interest not received until maturity, it is fully taxable each year.	$1,000 face value, but since purchased at discount, costs much lower.	Brokerage house Banks	From 2 to 5% of purchase price. Commission usually in price of bond. Minimum $38; then dependent on number of bonds; usually 1% of value.

INVESTMENT ALTERNATIVES (cont.)
MT=Medium-term / LT=Long-term

INVESTMENT	DEFINITION	RISK	TAX CONSEQUENCES	MINIMUM INVESTMENT	INSTITUTIONS OFFERING	COST
Unit trusts	Fixed portfolio of securities (municipal bonds, Ginnie Maes, corporate bonds, etc.). Receive interest/dividends monthly or semiannually and as each security matures, receive pro-rata share of redemption.	Fund is diversified, but not actively managed. Yields vary due to redemptions. Most trusts not insured. LT	Taxability determined by securities in trust.	1,000 units	Brokerage house Banks	Sales charge 3 to 5%. Mgmt. fee usually around 0.25%. May be included in price of unit. No transaction fees. Sales charge included in price of unit.
CMOs (collateralized mortgage obligations)	Pools of residential mortgages divided into maturity terms that determine when it will be repaid. Pays monthly: part interest, part return of principal.	Depends on issuer. Could be govt. agency, bank, builder. Hard to distinguish good from bad. MT, LT	Interest fully taxable. Return of capital not taxable.	$1,000	Brokerage house	Price includes commission of 0.5 to 3%.
Preferred stock	Security that pays high, fixed dividend, which must be paid before common stockholders can receive any	Dividend can be cut or eliminated. Price of stock falls if interest rates rise. LT	Dividends fully taxable. Capital gains fully taxable.	Stock prices vary.	Brokerage house	At full-service houses, per 100 shares: 2 to 4% of purchase price. At discount houses, 40 to 60% of full-service fees.

INVESTMENT ALTERNATIVES (*cont.*)

MT=Medium-term / LT=Long-term

Investment	Definition	Risk	Tax Consequences	Minimum Investment	Institutions Offering	Cost
Preferred stock (*cont.*)	dividend. If company liquidates, bonds paid back first, preferred stockholders next, common stock last. Price of securities rises much less than common stock.				Banks	40 to 60% of full-service brokerage house fees.
Common stock	Security that represents ownership in company. Share in profits and losses. Types include income, growth, blue chip, new issue. May or may not pay dividend.	Depends on type of stock, stock market conditions, economic climate. Last to collect if company liquidates. LT	Dividends fully taxable. Capital gains fully taxable.	Stock prices vary.	Brokerage house Banks	At full-service houses, 2 to 4% of purchase price. At discount houses, per 100 shares: 40 to 60% of full-service fees. Maximum charge $54 for first 100 shares plus $0.55 per share thereafter. Generally, 40 to 60% of full-service brokerage house fees.

The Investment Worksheet in this chapter will help you to create your own personal portfolio by matching your investments to your goals. Let's discuss the three steps involved.

STEP 1: DOLLAR COMMITMENT TO GOALS

First, state how much money you are committing to your goals in total. This will be the amount of additional cash flow you created in your budget. The next steps involve how much of this money you will allocate to each particular goal.

STEP 2: EMERGENCY FUND

Begin by determining how much of an emergency fund you need. Look at the total year's *fixed expense* figure from your Cash Flow Worksheet (pp. 53–55). Divide this number in half, and you'll have the amount you need to accumulate in this account. This is a *minimum* number. If you are married, and you and your spouse are working, this should be sufficient. However, if you are single and have no other means of support, you may feel more comfortable with a larger nest egg.

Next, fill in the target figures you will be aiming toward as you accumulate funds. This will determine how you will allocate the money.

Then, fill in the assets you *currently* have in each of the liquid investment categories.

Finally, determine how much of your additional cash flow from step 1 you will commit to funding your emergency fund. Write that amount on the line that corresponds to the investment you choose.

STEP 3: SHORT- AND MEDIUM-TERM GOALS (FEWER THAN FIVE YEARS)

List each of your goals in the blanks provided. Then quantify each goal, (put a dollar figure next to each one). Once again, fill in the assets you *currently* have for each goal and then put the amount you will commit to this fund each month for each investment vehicle. You may not use all the types I have listed, or you may include something I don't have. This is fine.

STEP 4: LONG-TERM GOALS (MORE THAN FIVE YEARS)

Repeat the same process from step 3, concentrating this time on your long-term goals.

STEP 5: INVESTMENT VEHICLES FOR EACH GOAL

Choose the appropriate investment or investments for your short-term and long-term goals. If you are not comfortable making that decision yet, you can accumulate the money in a savings account or money-market account while you educate yourself about the investment options or seek professional assistance. (This step is not on the worksheet.)

Let's take a look at Susan's Investment Worksheet. Reader, yours is on p. 98. Susan, were you able to come up with $1,000 more per month in cash flow?

SUSAN: Yes. I made a few changes in the habits I have, and I lowered my budget in three areas where I overspend the most: clothing, eating out, and vacations.

ANN: Terrific!

SUSAN: My fixed expenses are pretty high, so my emergency fund should have $35,000 to $40,000. I currently only have $2,500, but in case of an emergency, I could borrow from my 401(k) at work or get an additional loan on my apartment. However, I would rather not do that, so I will allocate $250 per month to the money-market fund for my emergency fund. That will add $3,000 this year and I will increase the amount in six months or when I get a raise. Once my money-market balance is over $10,000, I'll buy a Treasury bill.

ANN: Sounds good. What about your short-term goals?

SUSAN: Well, I'm going to concentrate on the down payment for the summer house, which we decided needed $477 per month for three years. After that, I will use that money to start my investment portfolio.

ANN: And your long-term goals?

SUSAN: Right now, I put about $5,000 per year into my 401(k) plan. I could put up to $9,000 per year in, and I would eventually like to do that. This year I am committed to increasing my contribution by $250 per month, or $3,000.

ANN: Great job, Susan. Does anyone have any comments?

Investment Worksheet

1. DOLLAR COMMITMENT TO GOALS
Amount of additional cash flow available/month: $ _____

2. EMERGENCY FUND Six months' fixed expenses $ _____

ALLOCATION	TARGETED AMOUNT	CURRENT BALANCE	AMOUNT COMMITTED TO FUND/MONTH
Cash			
Checking account			
Money-market fund			
CDs			
Treasury bills			

3. SHORT- AND MEDIUM-TERM GOALS (Fewer than five years)

	TARGETED AMOUNT	INVESTMENTS	CURRENT BALANCE	AMOUNT COMMITTED TO FUND/MONTH
Goal 1				
Goal 2				
Goal 3				

4. LONG-TERM GOALS (More than five years)

	TARGETED AMOUNT	INVESTMENTS	CURRENT BALANCE	AMOUNT COMMITTED TO FUND/MONTH
Goal 1				
Goal 2				
Goal 3				

Investment Worksheet

SUSAN

1. DOLLAR COMMITMENT TO GOALS
Amount of additional cash flow available/month: $ *1,000*

2. EMERGENCY FUND Six months' fixed expenses $ *35,000–40,000*

ALLOCATION	TARGETED AMOUNT	CURRENT BALANCE	AMOUNT COMMITTED TO FUND/MONTH
Cash			
Checking account	*2500*	*2500*	
Money-market fund	*12,500*		*250*
CDs			
Treasury bills	*25,000*		

3. SHORT- AND MEDIUM-TERM GOALS (Fewer than five years)

	TARGETED AMOUNT	INVESTMENTS	CURRENT BALANCE	AMOUNT COMMITTED TO FUND/MONTH
Summer house	*6,789*	*Bond mutual fund*	*5700*	*—*
Goal 1	*25,000*	*Borrow 401 (K)*	*25000*	*—*
$50,000	*18,211*	*Money Mkt.*	*0*	*477*
Investment portfolio Goal 2	*10,000/yr*	*?*	*0*	
Goal 3				

4. LONG-TERM GOALS (More than five years)

	TARGETED AMOUNT	INVESTMENTS	CURRENT BALANCE	AMOUNT COMMITTED TO FUND/MONTH
Retirement		*401(K) 50% global Fund 50% growth Fund*	*91,100*	*250*
Goal 1		*Pension*	*90,000*	
500,000		*IRA balanced Fund*	*12,800*	
Goal 2				
Goal 3				

JANE: Well, I have a question about this worksheet. If you're putting money toward a project and you are diversifying the investments, how do you decide which one to add to each month?

ANN: Let's say you have chosen three mutual funds for your retirement. If you divide each month's investment into the three funds, you will never have to guess which one is going to have the best performance that month. In addition, by putting the same amount into each fund you will be *dollar cost averaging.* This means that when the price of the shares is lower, you will be buying more shares that month, and when the price is higher, you will be buying fewer shares. Your average cost per share will always be lower than the current value in a rising market.

CAROL: You know what I like about that idea? There is nothing to think about. Once you decide on which funds to use, the money automatically goes into them each month.

TERRY: It almost sounds too simple. My mother always told me that if something sounds too easy, there is usually something wrong with it.

ANN: That may be true, but one of the reasons that people have difficulty investing their money is that they believe it's supposed to be complex. There is so much information published they get overwhelmed and paralyzed. They usually wind up doing nothing. This system of purchasing mutual funds may be boring to some people, but it's never boring to make money.

STACY: But what if you would like to buy individual stocks? Is there some way to get started?

ANN: Of course. Again, I would recommend taking a class to give you the basics. You could also read about it; see the list of financial resources in the back of this book (pp. 145–51).

One of the best ways to get started with ideas about which stocks to buy is to pay attention to what goods and services you or your children buy. For example, when my stepdaughter became a teenager, she was given a certain amount of money for her clothing allowance. She could spend it any way she wanted, but she had to stay within her budget. The first year we did this, I asked her where she went for her clothes. She told me she went to Benetton because that's where *all* the kids went, and the stuff was great. I immediately went out to buy Benetton stock, and sure enough, it did very well. The next year we went through this exercise again. This time she told me she went to the Gap because the clothes were "awesome" and much less expensive than Benetton, so she could buy much more. I sold my Benetton stock and bought the Gap, a very wise move, because

Benetton went down and the Gap went up a lot! Next time, she felt the Gap's inventory was not very appealing, but found clothes she liked at the Limited. Once again, I sold the Gap and bought the Limited. And once again, she was right on.

Of course, you cannot buy stocks solely based on what your children think is "in." What I am suggesting is that they will give you ideas that you can research. One popular way to learn more about stocks is to join an investment club. Each person in the club makes suggestions based on research (annual reports, newspaper and magazine articles, rating services, brokerage house reports), and the group votes on whether to add the stock to the portfolio. I have listed the addresses of two national investment club organizations on p. 150; they will send you information on how to organize your own group.

If you are using a full-service stockbroker, she will have research materials to help you, but if you're doing your own work, you will find a discount broker much more cost-effective. This type of broker does not give any advice; she just executes the transactions for you. The savings can be 40 to 60 percent off the regular commissions. Even if you're using a full-service broker, I would suggest asking for some discount if you have a reasonably large account and if you don't require too much time from her. The savings will *never* equal that of the discount broker, but then again the service is very different.

JANE: Are there some investments that are inappropriate once you get to a certain age?

ANN: As we get older we are more concerned with protecting our principal than we are in getting the highest return. Of course we still want to protect ourselves against inflation, and no one outgrows the desire to make money. However, we do not have the time required to recover a substantial loss that very speculative investments sometimes bring.

On the other hand, when we are young, we need to take some chances. This is not to say that you should gamble your money on a get-rich-quick scheme, but you should be open to opportunities with interesting potential.

TERRY: Wow! Do I have a great example to share relating to this! My sister was interviewing for a job that was only the second job she ever had. It was for a clothing manufacturer, and she liked the people very much. There seemed like a lot of promise, but they could only offer to pay her the same amount she was getting. She had heard somewhere that when you change jobs you're supposed to make more money, so she told them she would like to work there but needed to earn more. They said they were a new company and couldn't pay her more, but they would give her stock in the company, and if they made money, she would too. Later on, they would try to increase her pay. She decided to take another offer that seemed safer.

The company turned out to be Liz Claiborne, and now she checks out the price of the stock every day and makes herself crazy thinking how much she would have made!

ANN: What would have happened if she had taken the job and it didn't work out? Did she have people depending on her for income?

TERRY: No. She was single. I guess she would have gotten another job.

ANN: This is the perfect example of what I am talking about. You're right, Terry. She should have taken a chance. The consequences of its not working would not have been terrible. The same is true of a friend who is starting a business that you think could work out. Don't give her your last dollar, but maybe you want to participate in some way. It could turn out to be the next Apple Computer.

CAROL: Can we come back to my problem for a few minutes? I wish I had money to invest, but I don't even have money to pay my credit card bills. Is there some way to get out from under this mountain of debt so that I can someday have some investments?

ANN: We didn't forget about you, Carol. And believe me, you are *not* alone. In the next lesson, we will learn how to loosen the stranglehold of debt.

GETTING OUT OF DEBT

CAROL: You know, when I got divorced, I found myself in a very uncomfortable situation. My husband had used our credit cards up to the limit. I never owned a card on my own; I was always the secondary holder off of his credit. I found out that I had to requalify to get a card in my own name, yet I was responsible for the debts my husband had put on the existing card.

TERRY: That doesn't sound fair. If you're responsible for the debt, shouldn't you still have use of a card?

ANN: When you're going through a divorce, you're so traumatized it's hard to think clearly. However, it's imperative to separate the emotion from the reason. If you are legally separated or divorced, you should write to all credit card companies to close joint accounts in order to avoid liability on any charges your ex-husband makes. There are horror stories about women who followed their ex-husbands into bankruptcy; then it took the women years to re-establish their credit.

SUSAN: But what do you do about getting a credit card once you have canceled your joint cards?

ANN: You will need to reapply, and you may not qualify without your husband's income. This is why I suggest you establish your *own* credit history as soon as you can. If you're married and not working outside of the home, you can still be the primary holder of at least one of the credit cards that you and your husband possess. It's the primary holder who would keep the card in the case of divorce or death. If you apply for your own card and are told you need a co-signer, ask someone other than your husband, so that the record you are establishing is yours and not your husband's. If you had credit before you married, keep your individual cards and you will maintain your own history. You can also establish joint credit with your husband without losing your own.

JANE: My friend was traveling with her husband when he died in an accident. All their credit cards were in both their names, but she was not the primary holder of any of them. When she tried to use the cards for emergency airfare and to make arrangements, she could not use any of them. Money had to be sent to her.

ANN: That's another horrible example of what can happen if you don't have credit in your own name. Every woman should have the security of knowing that she has credit available in case of emergency.

STACY: How do you establish credit if you are just starting out?

ANN: The idea is to establish a history so that someone will want to extend credit to you. In order to do this, you first need to have a checking account that you keep in a responsible manner. This means not being overdrawn or bouncing checks. Having a savings account where you show a pattern of steady savings will also show fiscal responsibility.

Next, you open a charge account with a department store, which is easier to get than a national card. Make a few small purchases and pay them off before there is any finance charge. After a few months, you will probably find you are being solicited for a bank card, but if not, you can apply. Some find it helpful to take out a small personal loan with a bank and make prompt payments to show creditworthiness; however, in many cases this is not necessary.

SUSAN: I remember reading somewhere* that in order to get a credit card you need the three *c*'s, although I'm not sure I remember what they stand for. *Capacity, character,* and something else.

ANN: *Capacity, character,* and *collateral. Capacity* measures your earnings. Can you pay for this card? *Character* goes back to your history. Will you make the payments on a timely basis? And *collateral* looks to your assets and determines if the lender is covered in case you do not pay.

JANE: I know there's a scoring system the credit card companies use to decide whether you can be a cardholder. They look at things like your income and the amount of debt you already have, how long you have lived at your present address, and if you own your home or rent, and how well you paid your previous bills.

ANN: Each company has its own rating system. Sometimes you will be denied credit if the company feels you have too much credit already, or if there have been

* *Consumer Handbook to Credit Protection Laws.*

too many requests for credit checks. I had a young person in a seminar once who worked for a bank. She thought it was so cool that she could check her credit on a computer right where she worked that she became fixated on it, checking every week to see if anything changed. When she applied for a loan she was turned down. The reason: too many credit checks!

TERRY: I once applied for a card and was turned down. I felt mortified!

ANN: What did you do?

TERRY: What do you mean? What was there to do?

ANN: You could have requested an explanation. Under the Equal Credit Opportunity Act, you have a right to this information. There's a possibility the information they had received was incorrect. Even if there is just cause to deny you credit, at least you will know what you need to improve. And, of course, if you felt you were discriminated against because of sex or race, you can sue under the Equal Credit Opportunity Act. As a woman, you cannot be denied credit because you are married, single, divorced, or separated. A creditor may not request information about an ex-husband unless you are stating alimony as a source of income, or if you live in a community property state. You are entitled to a free copy of your credit report if you were denied credit because of something written in that report in the past 30 days. If you were not denied credit, but would like to see a copy of the report, you can request it from the credit bureau. (See p. 146 for the major national credit bureaus.) Some will send it free, others charge between $3 and $20 per report. When you request a copy, be sure to include your full name, Social Security number, date of birth, and addresses for the past five years.

JANE: When I was married, I had a card in my own name, Mrs. Thomas Jones. When I once requested a credit history, I found out that I didn't have one and I couldn't figure it out. It turned out that my history went into my husband's file because I used Mrs. Thomas Jones instead of Jane Jones.

ANN: Good point, Jane. When establishing your own credit, you want to be sure to use your own name.

SUSAN: How do you decide which card to take? There are so many, and I seem to get something in the mail every other day for another one.

ANN: First of all, you need to analyze how you'll be using the card. For instance, because I travel for my job, I need a lot of the services some cards provide: 24-hour replacement if stolen, insurance for my rental car, etc. For this reason, I have a card that charges a higher interest rate, in order to cover the expenses of these services. I rarely pay finance fees, so the higher interest rate doesn't bother me.

On the other hand, if you are using the card to spread out the payments of large purchases, look for a card with the lowest finance charges available.

TERRY: Isn't there also something about when they begin to charge interest that you have to be careful of?

ANN: Right. There are three methods for calculating your balance. In the *adjusted balance* method, the finance charges are added after subtracting all payments made during that period. If the yearly interest is 15 percent, the monthly interest rate is 1.25 percent (15% ÷ 12 = 1.25%). Let's say your previous balance was $500, and if you paid $300 during the month, you would be charged $2.50 interest ($500 − $300 = $200 × 1.25% = $2.50).

The second method is the *previous balance,* which does not subtract any payments made during the month. Therefore, in this instance, your interest would be $6.25 ($500 × 1.25% = $6.25).

The third method is the *average daily balance.* During the billing cycle, your balances are added up each day and then divided by the days in the month to determine the average. So, if your beginning balance was $500, and you paid $200 halfway through the month, you had 15 days of $500 balance, and 15 days of $300 balance, which averages to $5 interest charge ($400 × 1.25% = $5).

STACY: I had no idea there was any difference in how the interest is charged! What about these ads that say you can buy something now and not have to pay for six months. Is that legit?

SUSAN: My friend bought her furniture that way. What they didn't tell her was that although she wouldn't get a bill for six months, they were still computing the interest charges during that time. So when she did get her bill, it was much larger than she thought.

STACY: That's incredibly deceptive. Is that legal?

ANN: Buyer beware. You need to be an educated consumer and ask questions if a deal seems too good to be true. The Truth-in-Lending laws do demand that creditors tell you when the finance charges begin, but if they forget, you must be sure to remind them. The choices here are: from date of purchase, the average balance for the month, or a 25- to 30-day grace period before finance charges.

You must read *all* the information pertaining to the card you are getting. If there's no annual fee, make sure there's no mandatory loan attached to the application. What happens here is that as soon as you sign and send in the application, you receive a loan check in the mail whether or not you want it. Even if you pay it back within the month, the interest charge equals or exceeds what the annual fee would have been if you had to pay it.

CAROL

CAROL: My credit is a mess. I saw my credit report, and most of it was accurate, but there were a few items that were wrong. Does it pay to contact them, or will I open a can of worms?

ANN: Definitely contact them. There are various ways to clear your credit. (A booklet called *Consumer Credit Handbook* explains these matters in detail; see p. 145.) One is the dispute method. This works best if you have a clerical or computer error on your report, if the goods were damaged, if your card was stolen and someone made charges on it, etc. In this case you write directly to the credit bureau. They are legally required to investigate the item with the creditor. If they cannot verify the matter within 30 to 45 days, then by law the item must be removed from the credit report.

Regarding the accurate charges, there are several ways to proceed:

1. The Fair Credit Reporting Act states that certain items such as slow payment and nonpayment charges drop off your report after 7 years. Bankruptcies drop after 10 years. Obviously, this is not the quickest method, but if you haven't done anything about it for years and your time is almost up, this might be the easiest.

2. Negotiate directly with your creditors. Many times, you can agree to a

payment schedule or a settlement that will be satisfactory to them; in turn, they will keep the negative information off your credit report.

3. If you have tried everything and can get no relief, you can file a statement that will be attached to your credit report. In 100 words or less, you explain what happened to get you into this situation: for example, a medical emergency, loss of job, a move and the post office didn't forward your mail. At least the person reading the report will see your side of the story, and you have a chance at obtaining the credit you seek.

4. If you are in such trouble that you see no way out, I would suggest you contact the CCCS (Consumer Credit Counseling Service). This is a non-profit organization that will help you get in touch with your creditors, set up payment schedules, and counsel you on ways to avoid future problems. Their number is listed on p. 145.

CAROL: Does it make any sense to consolidate all my credit card debts into one loan with lower interest rates?

JANE: I know someone who did that and wound up losing her home!

ANN: She probably used an equity source loan, which uses a home as collateral. On the positive side, the interest you pay is tax deductible. On the negative side, if you don't make the payments, you can lose your home.

You may decide to consolidate all your debt into a lower cost personal loan where you don't get a tax deduction. What you do get is one bill to pay instead of numerous bills, and usually a lower interest rate. The problem is that it doesn't really address the underlying problem of overspending. Unless you cut up your credit cards, there is the danger that you will begin building balances on them again, and your credit crisis will worsen.

CAROL: Well, I could always go bankrupt and start over with a clean slate.

ANN: Bankruptcy should be considered *only* as a last resort. Not only does it remain on your credit report for 10 years, it can affect you for a much longer time. And another serious consequence is the way it makes you feel about yourself. People who work their way out of debt know they will never allow themselves to fall into that trap again. Those who give up and don't struggle to come back don't learn the lesson and have a very good chance of repeating the same mistakes.

STACY: What happens to you if your credit report is negative?

ANN: It's more like what *doesn't* happen to you. You may be denied a loan for a home, your prospective employer may order the report and decide you are not a good candidate for the job, you may not be able to rent an apartment or have the utility company connect your service without a large deposit.

STACY: If you clean it up, can you then get a credit card?

ANN: Negative information remains on your credit report for seven years. You may, however, be able to get a card before that, depending on the lender. There is also the possibility of obtaining a "secured" credit card.

STACY: What is that?

ANN: Remember when we discussed collateral as an area of concern for a credit card company? In order to assure themselves that there will be no problem in getting paid, the lender requires a deposit equal to your line of credit on the card. That way, if you don't pay, the money is withdrawn from your account.

TERRY: How much debt is too much debt?

ANN: Again, it depends on the individual, but as a guideline, I would say you should keep your consumer debt payments down to 10 to 15 percent of your *net monthly income* after taxes are paid. Consumer interest payments, which include credit card, personal, school, and car loans (it excludes mortgage payments), are *not* tax deductible anymore, so the government is not helping you foot the bill.

   To determine if you are within the guidelines turn to the Too Much Debt? Worksheet on p. 111. Carol, may we use you as an example to help us understand these sheets, since your number one goal is to work out your debt situation?

CAROL: Sure, why not? You already know more about my troubles than my mother does. If it can get me to a place where I can understand how to work it out myself, it will be a lifesaver.

ANN: Thanks, Carol. Not only will you be helping yourself, you will be helping others in the same predicament. Let's fill in the sheet.

STEP 1

   Make a list of your charge accounts and consumer loans (consumer loans include auto, education, and personal loans). State the payment you make monthly on each of the cards or loans, and come up with a total. Carol's is $450 per month.

STEP 2

   Write your net monthly income. (You can get this number from your budget sheets.) Calculate 10 percent of your monthly income; then 15 percent. Carol's monthly net income is $2,250. And 10 percent of that is $225; 15 percent is $337.50.

Too Much Debt? Worksheet

I. DEBTS

CHARGE ACCOUNTS	PAYMENT/MONTH
Gasoline Card	$ 50
Department Store Card	100
National Charge Card	150

CONSUMER LOANS	
Auto Loan	$ 150

TOTAL: $ 450   A

2. NET MONTHLY INCOME $ 2,250

10% of net monthly income $ 225   B
15% of net monthly income $ 337.50   C

3. SUMMARY

A $ 450   vs. B $ 225

A $ 450   vs. C $ 337.50

Too Much Debt? Worksheet

1. DEBTS

CHARGE ACCOUNTS	PAYMENT/MONTH
_____	$ _____
_____	_____
_____	_____
_____	_____
_____	_____

CONSUMER LOANS	
_____	$ _____
_____	_____
_____	_____

TOTAL: $ _____ **A**

2. NET MONTHLY INCOME $ _____

10% of net monthly income $ _____ **B**
15% of net monthly income $ _____ **C**

3. SUMMARY

A $ _____   vs. **B** $ _____

A $ _____   vs. **C** $ _____

STEP 3

Compare the amount you are currently paying to the results in step 2. (Compare line A versus B; then line A versus C.) Carol pays more than 15 percent of her monthly net income, in fact, she pays 20 percent.

CAROL: No wonder I can't make any headway. And since I'm paying only the minimum balances, I'll *never* be able to pay these debts off completely.

ANN: I agree with you. We need to develop a plan of timely payment that will enable you to become debt-free within a reasonable period of time. A friend of mine, Robert Ortalda, Jr., developed a very effective system that he kindly has agreed to let me include in this workbook.* I'm so pleased, because it does illustrate beautifully the importance of paying off more than the minimum balance on your credit cards. So let's move on to the Debt Description Worksheet. Once again, Carol, we'll use your case as our example.

STEP 1

Describe the debt, the total amount owed, the interest rate charged on each debt, and the amount of the minimum payment. Also note if there's a special characteristic, such as a loan owed to parents or if the debt is to be paid back whenever possible, etc.

STEP 2

Target the debt that costs you the most in interest to pay off first. If you have two debts with the same interest rate, concentrate on the one with the lower balance. In your case, Carol, this is the 18 percent credit card with a $2,000 balance. You're currently paying $100 per month on your minimum balance. How long would it take you to pay this off if you did not charge anything additional on this card and continued to pay only $100 per month?

Look at the table titled Number of Monthly Payments Required to Retire Debt (pp. 116–17). Across the top, there are percentages that represent the interest rate you're paying on the debt. Look for 18 percent. You now need to figure out how much of the debt you're paying off each month. You pay $100 on $2,000 (100 divided by 2,000 equals .05 or 5 percent). Look for 5 percent down the left-hand

---

* Robert Ortalda, Jr.,'s book *How to Live Within Your Means and Still Finance Your Dreams* describes a system of budgeting and funding.

Debt Description Worksheet

DEBT	AMOUNT OWED	INTEREST RATE	MINIMUM PAYMENT/MONTH
Charge Accounts			
_____	_____	_____	_____
_____	_____	_____	_____
_____	_____	_____	_____
_____	_____	_____	_____
Consumer Loans			
_____	_____	_____	_____
_____	_____	_____	_____
_____	_____	_____	_____
Education Loans			
_____	_____	_____	_____
_____	_____	_____	_____
Personal Loans			
_____	_____	_____	_____
_____	_____	_____	_____
		TOTAL:	_____

Debt Description Worksheet

CAROL

DEBT	AMOUNT OWED	INTEREST RATE	MINIMUM PAYMENT/MONTH
Charge Accounts			
Gasoline Card	1500	16	50
Department Store Card	2000	18	100
National Charge Card	5000	18	150
Consumer Loans			
Auto	2500	10	150
Education Loans			
Personal Loans			
Parents	2500	0	—
		TOTAL:	450

column of the chart. Follow the line across until you come to the 18 percent column. They intersect at 24 months.

Carol, when you did your cash flow, budgeting, and investment worksheets you came up with an additional $100 per month to dedicate to funding, as I recall. You take that $100 and add it to the amount you are already paying on this card. So now, instead of $100, you will pay $200 per month. On a $2,000 bill, $200 per month is 10 percent of the bill, right? Now check the chart. See where the 10 percent payment and the 18 percent interest charge intersect and you'll discover that this bill can be paid off in 10.9 months instead of 24 months. This means that you're free of this debt more than 13 months sooner!

STEP 3

Even though you are concentrating your additional cash flow on the $2,000 debt, you are continuing to pay the minimum balances on your other debts. Now, after 11 months, you have totally paid off the first card. Set your sights on the second target: the $5,000 debt at 18 percent. After 11 months of paying the $150 minimum you will have a balance of approximately $4,100 (see the table on p. 118). If you continue to pay $150 per month, you can see from the table on pp. 116–17 that it will take you about 37 months to pay this off entirely (150 ÷ 4,100 = 3.6%). Instead, Carol, you will now pay $150 (what you currently pay) plus $200 (the amount you were paying on the previous bill that you completed), which equals $350. This new monthly payment is approximately 8.5% (350 ÷ 4,100) of the balance. Checking the chart again, we see that you cut the payment time down on this bill from 37 months to 13 months—that is from more than three years to a little over one year.

STEP 4

Your next highest interest rate is your department store credit card at 16 percent. Here you owe $1,500, and you have been paying $50 per month for the two years you were concentrating on your two highest interest rate cards (11 months for the department store card in step 2, and 13 months for the national charge card in step 3). You would have paid off about half of this $1,500 debt in that two-year period by paying $50 per month. Since $50 is about 6.7 percent of the $750 balance (50 ÷ 750), the chart shows us that continuing at this rate it would take between 16 and 17.3 months to complete. However when you pay $50 (what you pay now) plus $350 (what you had been devoting to the other charge accounts), you put $400 toward the bill, which is 53 percent of the bill. You are finished in just two months!

NUMBER OF MONTHLY PAYMENTS REQUIRED TO RETIRE DEBT

PAYMENT AS % OF DEBT	STATED ANNUAL INTEREST RATE OF DEBT									
	5%	6%	7%	8%	9%	10%	11%	12%	13%	14%
1.0%	129.6	139.0	150.5	165.3	185.5	215.9	272.3	*	*	*
1.5%	78.3	81.3	84.7	88.5	92.8	97.7	103.5	110.4	118.9	129.7
2.0%	56.2	57.7	59.3	61.0	62.9	64.9	67.2	69.7	72.4	75.5
2.5%	43.8	44.7	45.7	46.7	47.7	48.9	50.1	51.3	52.7	54.2
3.0%	36.0	36.6	37.2	37.8	38.5	39.2	40.0	40.7	41.6	42.5
3.5%	30.5	30.9	31.3	31.8	32.3	32.8	33.3	33.8	34.4	35.0
4.0%	26.5	26.8	27.1	27.4	27.8	28.2	28.5	28.9	29.3	29.7
4.5%	23.4	23.6	23.9	24.1	24.4	24.7	25.0	25.3	25.6	25.9
5.0%	20.9	21.1	21.3	21.5	21.8	22.0	22.2	22.4	22.7	22.9
5.5%	18.9	19.1	19.3	19.4	19.6	19.8	20.0	20.2	20.4	20.6
6.0%	17.3	17.4	17.6	17.7	17.9	18.0	18.2	18.3	18.5	18.6
6.5%	15.9	16.0	16.2	16.3	16.4	16.5	16.7	16.8	16.9	17.1
7.0%	14.8	14.9	15.0	15.1	15.2	15.3	15.4	15.5	15.6	15.7
7.5%	13.7	13.8	13.9	14.0	14.1	14.2	14.3	14.4	14.5	14.6
8.0%	12.9	12.9	13.0	13.1	13.2	13.3	13.3	13.4	13.5	13.6
8.5%	12.1	12.2	12.2	12.3	12.4	12.4	12.5	12.6	12.7	12.7
9.0%	11.4	11.5	11.5	11.6	11.6	11.7	11.8	11.8	11.9	12.0
9.5%	10.8	10.8	10.9	11.0	11.0	11.1	11.1	11.2	11.2	11.3
10.0%	10.2	10.3	10.3	10.4	10.4	10.5	10.5	10.6	10.6	10.7
11.0%	9.3	9.3	9.4	9.4	9.5	9.5	9.5	9.6	9.6	9.7
12.0%	8.5	8.5	8.6	8.6	8.6	8.7	8.7	8.7	8.8	8.8
13.0%	7.8	7.9	7.9	7.9	8.0	8.0	8.0	8.0	8.1	8.1
14.0%	7.3	7.3	7.3	7.3	7.4	7.4	7.4	7.4	7.5	7.5
15.0%	6.8	6.8	6.8	6.8	6.9	6.9	6.9	6.9	7.0	7.0
20.0%	5.1	5.1	5.1	5.1	5.1	5.1	5.1	5.2	5.2	5.2
25.0%	4.0	4.1	4.1	4.1	4.1	4.1	4.1	4.1	4.1	4.1
30.0%	3.4	3.4	3.4	3.4	3.4	3.4	3.4	3.4	3.4	3.4
35.0%	2.9	2.9	2.9	2.9	2.9	2.9	2.9	2.9	2.9	2.9
40.0%	2.5	2.5	2.5	2.5	2.5	2.5	2.5	2.5	2.5	2.6
45.0%	2.2	2.2	2.2	2.2	2.2	2.3	2.3	2.3	2.3	2.3

* Payment results in negative amortization: Loan never gets repaid because principal balance rises each month, instead of falling.

15%	16%	17%	18%	19%	20%	21%	22%
*	*	*	*	*	*	*	*
144.2	165.9	205.5	*	*	*	*	*.
79.0	82.9	87.6	93.1	99.9	108.4	119.9	136.9
55.8	57.5	59.4	61.5	63.9	66.5	69.4	72.8
43.4	44.4	45.4	46.6	47.8	49.1	50.5	52.0
35.6	36.2	36.9	37.6	38.3	39.1	40.0	40.8
30.2	30.6	31.1	31.6	32.1	32.6	33.2	33.7
26.2	26.5	26.9	27.2	27.6	28.0	28.4	28.8
23.2	23.4	23.7	24.0	24.2	24.5	24.8	25.1
20.8	21.0	21.2	21.4	21.6	21.8	22.1	22.3
18.8	19.0	19.1	19.3	19.5	19.7	19.9	20.1
17.2	17.3	17.5	17.6	17.8	17.9	18.1	18.2
15.8	16.0	16.1	16.2	16.3	16.5	16.6	16.7
14.7	14.8	14.9	15.0	15.1	15.2	15.3	15.4
13.7	13.8	13.9	13.9	14.0	14.1	14.2	14.3
12.8	12.9	13.0	13.0	13.1	13.2	13.3	13.4
12.0	12.1	12.2	12.2	12.3	12.4	12.5	12.5
11.4	11.4	11.5	11.5	11.6	11.7	11.7	11.8
10.7	10.8	10.9	10.9	11.0	11.0	11.1	11.1
9.7	9.8	9.8	9.8	9.9	9.9	10.0	10.0
8.9	8.9	8.9	9.0	9.0	9.0	9.1	9.1
8.1	8.2	8.2	8.2	8.3	8.3	8.3	8.4
7.5	7.6	7.6	7.6	7.6	7.7	7.7	7.7
7.0	7.0	7.1	7.1	7.1	7.1	7.2	7.2
5.2	5.2	5.2	5.2	5.3	5.3	5.3	5.3
4.1	4.1	4.1	4.2	4.2	4.2	4.2	4.2
3.4	3.4	3.4	3.4	3.5	3.5	3.5	3.5
2.9	2.9	2.9	2.9	2.9	3.0	3.0	3.0
2.6	2.6	2.6	2.6	2.6	2.6	2.6	2.6
2.3	2.3	2.3	2.3	2.3	2.3	2.3	2.3

CAROL'S REPAYMENT SCHEDULE ON NATIONAL CHARGE CARD

$5,000 principal; simple interest at 1.5% per month (18% per year)

MONTH	OUTSTANDING BALANCE	TOTAL PAYMENT	INTEREST	APPLIED TO PRINCIPAL	NEW BALANCE
1	$5,000.00	$150.00	$75.00	$75.00	$4,925.00
2	4,925.00	150.00	73.88	76.12	4,848.88
3	4,848.88	150.00	72.73	77.27	4,771.61
4	4,771.61	150.00	71.57	78.43	4,693.18
5	4,693.18	150.00	70.40	79.60	4,613.58
6	4,613.18	150.00	69.20	80.80	4,532.78
7	4,532.78	150.00	67.99	82.01	4,450.77
8	4,450.77	150.00	66.76	83.24	4,367.53
9	4,367.53	150.00	65.51	84.49	4,283.04
10	4,283.04	150.00	64.25	85.75	4,197.29
11	4,197.29	150.00	62.96	87.04	4,110.25

STEP 5

Here's the best part. When you've finished with all the old debts, and if you are careful not to incur new ones that are not funded within your budget, you will have $400 per month to put away toward something that you *really want*! If you save $400 per month, you'll save $4,800 per year. Earning 6 percent interest, that would grow to $27,058 in 5 years, $63,264 in 10 years, and $263,349 in 25 years. Are you impressed? Carol, what do you think?

CAROL: I can't believe it. In a little more than two years, I can be out from under this mountain of debt. I thought it would take me a lifetime. By that time even my car will be paid off, so the only money I will still owe is the loan from my parents. I *know* I can do this.

ANN: Of course you can do it. Reader, it's time for you to fill in your Debt Description Worksheet (p. 113). Use the table on pp. 116–17, and if you have any problems, review Carol's example once more.

TERRY: I have a student loan with a low interest payment. Should I apply this same principle and pay it off, or should I just continue to pay it as I have in the past?

ANN: If the interest rate is less than you could earn on the money by investing it, you should just continue to pay it every month. However, when the rates you have to pay are 15 percent, or 18 percent, these are amounts we cannot earn without taking a lot of risk. At these high rates I know of no better investment than to pay off your debts. Especially considering the fact that you cannot take the interest you pay as a tax deduction on consumer-type loans.

SUSAN: It's amazing how much of our cash flow goes to pay off old things that as you said before we have probably already thrown away.

ANN: That's why we want to turn the process around and allocate money to the items we want, even the indulgences, so we are always *in control* of what we are spending our money on.

STACY: I have an odd question. I owe my parents $1,300 that I borrowed to take a trip before I started work. They are charging me no interest and told me to just pay it back when I could. I feel guilty about this, but because I don't have to pay any interest, I don't feel a pressing need to pay them.

ANN: There is an important lesson to learn from this. If you need to borrow money, the cheapest interest rates (many times 0 percent) can be found with parents or close relatives. This is obviously beneficial to the borrower, and, Stacy, you are absolutely right, according to the method of repayment we have just discussed, you would pay this bill off last. However, if you are the lender, I would suggest you *always* ask for interest. Why? Because then maybe you have a chance at getting paid back someday.

SUSAN: If only I had met you before I lent my brother that $25,000 down payment for his house. His timing was perfect—I had gotten a bonus for a huge account I brought into the office. He keeps saying he will pay me back, but it's been three years and I haven't seen a nickel yet. Of course, I told him not to worry about any interest.

ANN: I suspect the next time you are in this situation, you will rethink how you handle it. You may decide to do it exactly the same way, and this is fine, as long as you are consciously making that decision. You never want to lend money and then feel resentful later.

I saw the light of understanding flash on many of your faces during this lesson. I hope it is all coming together for you. Assuming control of your finances takes time, but working on it a little at a time will get the job done. You have all made a great start.

LESSON 14

PLANNING FOR RETIREMENT

■■ ■■ ■■

JANE: Now that I have all my worksheets, I have a very good idea of where my finances are right now. But how do I know if I can retire now or if I need to accumulate more resources?

ANN: Jane, since retirement planning was your objective when you began this seminar, let's complete the following Planning Your Retirement Worksheet with your information. Is that OK with you?

JANE: Absolutely. I need all the help I can get.

ANN: Good. First, how do you picture your retirement?

JANE: Since this was my number one goal, I've given it a lot of thought. I've decided *not* to move for the time being, since I'm not sure where I would like to live. For the next few years, I want to travel to various locations that are possibilities and spend a month in each to see how I like it. When I think I've found the right place, I'll rent an apartment there for a few months before I buy.

SUSAN: That's really sensible. My mother bought an apartment in Florida as soon as she retired and discovered later it was not the best area for her. If she had rented first, she would have saved a lot of aggravation. It's also a good idea to visit in the off-season to see if you want to be there all year before you sell your home.

JANE: Actually, I'm thinking of getting a smaller place here so I can be around the family in the summer, and going south only for the winter. I also want to devote more time to the community hospital, where I volunteer now once a week. I have been asked to be chairperson of all volunteers, and as soon as I retire, I'd have the time.

JANE

CAROL: Have you definitely decided that you'll stop working?

JANE: Actually, no. For the first few years, at least, I would like to work part-time. I've been a legal secretary for many years, and the firm I work with has been very supportive. They have agreed to let me work on a consulting basis—I can make my own schedule, as long as I'm flexible during the times they are very busy.

ANN: It is so important while you are making a transition to stay open to possibilities. I like the idea that you will not completely stop working but will ease out gradually, because the change is not so extreme. It also keeps you in contact with the people you have spent time with over the years.

SUSAN: I always thought when I retired, I'd just want to lie in a hammock, sip a drink, and read all those novels I never had time for when I was working.

ANN: That's what many people think. The problem is, what do you do after six months when you've read all the novels, or seen all the movies, or gone to lunch with all your girlfriends? Everyone thinking of retirement should list what she does each hour of the day now, while she is working, and then fill in what she plans to do when she stops working. If the first sheet is totally filled up, and the second sheet has a lot of white space, then retirement will be a difficult adjustment. You can't go from being busy every minute of the day to having nothing to do. This is not to say that every minute has to be accounted for, but it does mean that a plan is important.

JANE: This is definitely *not* an overnight decision for me. I have thought long and hard about what I want to do. But even if I don't do it tomorrow, I want to know if I *can* do it. It would give me peace of mind to know that when I'm ready, my finances will be ready too.

ANN: Fine. Let's discuss the areas we need to explore, and then we'll construct a worksheet to put it all together.

First, we want to examine any area that may provide retirement income: *Social Security, employer plans,* and *personal investments.*

STACY: How long do you have to work to qualify for Social Security? I'm going to have to contribute for 40-plus years before I see any benefits, right? I hear people say there won't be any Social Security by the time I retire.

ANN: If you're married and your husband is injured or dies, there are disability and survivor benefits that Social Security will pay before retirement, but of course we hope this won't be the case. For our discussion now, let's limit ourselves to the retirement benefits you collect if you have contributed for 40 quarters. (That's the same as a total of 10 years, though the years don't necessarily have to be in a row. And if you were born before 1929, it will be less.) The actual amount you will receive is determined by how long you have worked, the amount you have earned while working, and your age at retirement.

As for Stacy's question about whether there will be a Social Security fund around in decades to come, it probably won't be eliminated, but it may exist in a different form from today. As more of us age, and if we don't produce more children, there will be fewer contributors for the amount of revenue needed. This will result in a decline in benefits, an increase in taxes, or a raising of the age when you can begin to collect.

JANE: I sent away to Social Security for a copy of my earnings and benefit statement, which estimated how much I would receive at retirement at three different ages. It was very easy to do . All I had to fill out was my name, Social Security number, and the amount I expected to earn in the next year. I told them both my name before and after marriage to ensure that my entire working career would be credited. The earnings and benefit statement came back with the amount I had contributed to the fund since I began working. I also requested my husband's benefit, because I believe I am entitled to his money also.

ANN: Actually, you have a choice. While you are both alive, a spouse is entitled to her full benefit or one-half of her spouse's, whichever is higher. If you are receiving the 50 percent payment as a spouse and your husband dies, you will then be entitled to receive your husband's full benefit. (Any married woman who collects her own full benefit is also, once her husband dies, entitled to *his* full benefit instead of her own. A woman who is not yet 60 and is collecting the benefits of her deceased husband may lose those benefits if she remarries. If you remarry after age 60, generally you will be able to receive benefits either from your deceased spouse or your new one, whichever man's is higher.) It was smart to request both figures so you'll be able to see which is more beneficial for you. I'm glad you already have this information from Social Security, Jane, so that we'll be able to use accurate figures for our worksheet. For anyone who has not sent in for this information, you should do it every three years, so that if there's a mistake it can be remedied. To have Form SSA-7004-PC (Request for Earnings and Benefit Estimate Statement) sent to you, call 800-772-1213.

CAROL: Can I get benefits based on my ex-husband's earnings, or did I lose them when we got divorced?

ANN: If you were married for at least 10 years, which you were, Carol, you *are* eligible for half of your ex-husband's benefits when you reach age 62, as long as your ex-husband is 62 and eligible to receive benefits and you are unmarried when the application is filed. Even if he remarries, you (and his current wife) are entitled to the benefits.

TERRY: I remember when my mother got her Social Security benefits. I was amazed at how small her distribution was.

ANN: To find out why, we would need to analyze your mother's work history. But realize that Social Security is supposed to be just *one* source of income in retirement; not the *only* source. Many women who take time off from work to raise their family find that their Social Security is reduced because they have contributed less to the fund.

JANE: If I retired now instead of waiting until I'm 65, would I receive significantly less money? And what if I continue to work after age 65? Shouldn't I wait to take my Social Security benefit until I actually do retire?

ANN: If you retire now, at age 62, you would receive 80 percent of your total benefit at age 65. Since you're receiving the money three years earlier and can currently use it, it would take you a number of years of the higher payments (at age 65) to equal what you have already received. However, if you continue to work at age 62 and collect your benefit, you will lose $1 in benefits for every $2 earned over $7,680.* If you are age 65, continue to work, and collect your benefit, you lose $1 in benefits for every $3 earned over $10,560. If you continue to work past age 70 and collect your benefit, you can earn an unlimited amount without losing any benefits.

Jane, if you continue to work until age 65, wait to collect your Social Security so you don't get penalized for earning over the threshold. It's very possible that you will collect your Social Security for 20 to 35 years, so why receive a reduced benefit?

At 65, you can make a decision, but if you work part-time, you will probably try to remain within the allowed threshold of $10,560. (The amount you are allowed to earn goes up each year by the percentage increase in the consumer price index, which is a calculation measuring the rise in inflation.)

Remember, you must apply to receive your benefits; they are not automatically sent to you. It takes two to three months to begin receiving the checks, which can be deposited directly into your bank account.

TERRY: I'm confused. You mean you can have an income of only $10,560 when you are getting Social Security at age 65 or you will lose benefits?

ANN: You can *earn* only $10,560. Unearned income (interest, dividends, capital gains, etc.) does not reduce benefits. Let's take an example of a 62-year-old person who has $40,000 in dividend and interest payments and has a job where she earns $20,000. At 62, she will lose $1 for every $2 earned over $7,680 ($20,000 − $7,680 = $12,320). Therefore, she will lose $6,160 of her Social Security benefit. Depending on how much her total benefit is, if she earns over a certain amount of money, the total benefit could be lost, and there would be no point in filing for it.

CAROL: Is Social Security taxed? Hasn't this money already been taxed?

ANN: In the past, Social Security was not taxed. However, now if your adjusted gross income, your nontaxable income (tax-free bonds), and one half of your Social Security adds up to $25,000 ($32,000 for a couple), you will pay tax on your Social Security. You see, modifications have already been made to the system to compensate for increased amounts of outgo.

CAROL: I knew Social Security was complex, but I had no idea it was this confusing.

ANN: There are a lot of rules, but once you're ready to retire, you can call or visit Social Security and they will work out your individual benefits for you.

For now, we want an estimate of how much we'll get per year upon retirement.

* The figures in this section are accurate as of the time this book went to press.

The first step is sending the form to Social Security to obtain your benefit information. The details should be worked out closer to your retirement date.

Now, let's move on to the second source of income, employer plans.

SUSAN: When I asked the employee benefit people for my statement, I received one for my 401(k) plan, one for a defined benefit plan, which I don't understand, and one for the company stock plan. Are these all considered retirement plans?

ANN: Yes. They are all forms of plans offered by your employer. Like Susan, any of you who work at a company that has any type of plan should contact the employee benefits department or human resources department to find out what you will be entitled to upon retirement. They will not be able to give you specific figures, but they will give you a document explaining the benefits, at what age you become eligible, how to calculate what you'll receive, etc. Also, be sure that you're not overlooking plans from previous jobs that may still be in effect.

STACY: Can you explain the difference between the types of plans?

ANN: Sure. Basically there are two types: *defined benefit* and *defined contribution*. A defined benefit plan has a formula based on your earnings and years of service. The company guarantees you a certain amount of benefit per year. This type of plan is not common now because companies do not like to be locked into fixed payouts.

The more popular type is a defined contribution plan. A percentage of your pay is put aside by the company, and the amount you get upon retirement is determined by the amount of the contributions and how the money is invested. The most popular of these plans is the 401(k), or the salary-reduction plan. In this plan, every dollar you contribute reduces your federal taxable income by the same amount. Many corporations will match their employees' contributions up to a certain percentage. What this means is that if you put in $1, and your company puts in $0.25, you have made 25 percent on your investment, a terrific return that is added to your fund even *before* the money is invested!

Another type of defined contribution plan is a profit-sharing plan. Here the company contributes if there's a profit for the year. In the lean years, there may be no contribution.

STACY: My company has a 401(k) plan, which I'm going to participate in when I'm hired full-time, and they do match my contribution up to a certain percentage. But there's something about their money being vested over a number of years. I'm not clear on what that means.

ANN: That means that if you left your job after a year, you would be entitled to the money that you contributed to the plan but *not* the money the firm contributed.

This is done to encourage you to remain with the company. You have to check your particular plan for the vesting schedule, since each will differ. However, according to the Employees' Retirement Income Security Act (ERISA), the broad rules are that the employer's portion can vest all at once (100%) after five years, or it can be phased in at 20 percent after three years, and 20 percent per year thereafter, with total vesting after seven years.

STACY: Let me understand this. I stay at my job for three years, and I have $2,000 in the 401(k) and my company has put in $500. Then I decide to leave. I keep my $2,000 because that is *my* money, but I only get 20 percent of the firm's $500, or $100?

ANN: Yes, if your vesting schedule is the 20 percent phase-in kind. If it is the all-at-once type, you wouldn't get *any* of the $500. You would have had to be at the firm for five years.

JANE: I've been at my firm for 25 years, so I'm totally vested in my 401(k) plan. In addition, I have a small pension. Susan mentioned a stock plan that she has at her company. What's that?

ANN: Many large firms may either offer employees stock in the company at favorable rates or give stock as a bonus or incentive. It motivates employees to work hard for profits in their company.

TERRY: When we were doing our inventories, I asked my husband about his pension. He started to explain something about the different ways he would take his money when he retired. When my eyes started to glaze, he realized I didn't understand and said we would discuss it at another time. Do you know what he might have been talking about?

ANN: Many plans give you a choice of how you can receive your money. One way would be in the form of an annuity, where you receive monthly payments for life, or for a specified time period.

CAROL: Why would you choose a certain time period, if you could get it for life?

ANN: In this case, when the payment is for life, it's only for the life of the recipient. When that person dies, even if she dies before receiving one payment, no additional money is paid out to her heirs. However, if she takes an annuity for a certain period of time, her heirs would receive the payments even if the retiree died immediately.

TERRY: What would happen to a wife if the husband took an annuity on his life and he died? She would get nothing?

ANN: That's right. But the laws protect spouses. A husband (or wife) can take an annuity on his life *only* if the spouse grants permission in writing.

TERRY: But why would anyone sign that?

ANN: What if a wife is retiring and she is 20 years younger than her husband. They are financially secure, and they determine that the wife will, in all probability, outlive the husband. They might opt for the higher payment she would receive in taking the individual life option, so she would receive the most money possible. Or a couple might choose the higher payment and put the additional money they would be receiving into a life insurance policy for the spouse's use in case of death.

Because there are so many choices, it's imperative to sit down and map out a strategy before you make these decisions. For the time being, let's use the figures from our employee benefits to determine where we stand right now. This will help you to develop your plan.

SUSAN: Before we leave this topic, may I ask one more question? A colleague of mine is leaving our firm and she told me she is taking her 401(k) and "rolling it over." What exactly is she doing?

ANN: When you leave a job, sometimes you can continue to have your money invested in the company plan until retirement, or you can take it out in a lump sum. If you just take the money and put it with your personal investments, or spend it, you will be taxed. (Remember, this is money that has not been taxed before.) If you do this prior to age $59\frac{1}{2}$, you'll pay tax *plus* a penalty of 10 percent for taking it before retirement. So in order to avoid paying taxes and penalties, most people "roll the money over" into a rollover IRA, which is another type of retirement plan that allows accumulations without paying taxes until the money is withdrawn at retirement. This money can be put into a mutual fund, a brokerage account, a bank, an annuity—anything designating it as a retirement account that is not being used currently. If you are leaving a firm and are going to roll over your account, make sure that you have your company transfer the money *directly* to the new account within 60 days. If you personally take the money (even if you roll it over yourself), you'll have to pay 20 percent withholding to the government.

CAROL: I never worked anywhere long enough to qualify for any kind of pension from an employer.

ANN: You're not the only one. Many people cannot count on their employment as a resource; all the more reason to take responsibility for financing your own retirement. Which leads us to the third source of income for retirement: our individual retirement plans and personal savings.

SUSAN: I haven't contributed to my IRA since I began participating in my 401(k) because I no longer get a tax deduction. Is that right?

ANN: You're right that you don't get the tax deduction if you have a plan at work and earn over a certain amount of money ($25,000 single, $40,000 joint). But an

IRA (individual retirement account) still allows you to accumulate money on a tax-deferred basis, which means you pay no taxes on the *appreciation* until retirement. If you were going to save an additional $2,000 toward your retirement anyway, aren't you better off doing it in an account where you pay no taxes?

SUSAN: I don't know. I couldn't get my hands on the money in case of an emergency without paying a penalty.

ANN: True. That's a disadvantage. But in a true emergency, you probably are not going to be that concerned with the penalty. On the other hand, you will *not* be willing to pay the penalty to withdraw the money for a nonemergency item, like a vacation or a new car. If you have $10,000 in an IRA, and earn 6 percent on the money, you will earn $600 and keep the entire amount in the account. If you have $10,000 in your personal account and earn the same amount, Susan, you will pay taxes of 28 percent, or $168. (Reader, check your tax bracket for the amount you will have to pay to the government.) This leaves $432, which will be further reduced if you live in a place where you pay state and city taxes. Why keep only a portion of the $600 when you can keep the entire amount?

STACY: What if you can only do one plan? Are you better off doing the one at work?

ANN: Yes. First, if they match your contribution, you are obviously at an advantage. Second, they usually provide investment management for the funds.

TERRY: I'm not working right now. I can't have an IRA, can I?

ANN: To make a contribution to an IRA you must have *earned* income. However, there is something called a spousal IRA, which allows the working spouse to make a total contribution of $2,250. This money can be divided into separate accounts between the spouses any way they choose.

TERRY: If I start a business at home, then I can do an IRA?

ANN: You have to earn some money first, but sure you can. In fact, if you earn *only* $2,000, you could put the entire amount in an IRA if you want. However, if your business begins to be very profitable, you would want to open a Keogh account. This is a retirement plan for self-employed people that allows you to put up to 20 percent of your net income into a tax-deferred account, up to a maximum of $30,000 per year.

SUSAN: I earn some money as a director of a small company. Is this considered my own business and can I open a Keogh based on this income?

ANN: Absolutely. Many people start small businesses and take some of the money they earn specifically to establish another retirement plan for themselves. You can

Planning Your Retirement Worksheet

1. Present annual gross income before taxes $ _____

2. Annual gross income prior to retirement (use Future Value Table, p. 80) _____

3. Annual retirement income needed (step 2 multiplied by 80%) _____

4. Assuming 5% inflation rate, the annual income you will need to retire (step 3 times multiplier in Future Value Table) _____

5. Estimated Social Security _____

6. Expected annual pension _____

7. Expected income from 401(k) or other employer plan _____

8. Estimated savings and investments expected at retirement that will provide income or be drawn from your principal _____

9. Estimated retirement income per year you can expect from your savings in step 8 _____

10. Add items in steps 5, 6, 7, and 9, and then subtract step 4. _____

11. If step 10 is a negative number (shortfall in the amount needed per year to retire), divide the shortfall by the percentage you estimate you could earn if this shortfall were invested. _____

12. Divide the result in step 11 by the appropriate annuity factor from the Annuity Factors Table (p. 82) table to determine how much you need to save each year from now to retirement to obtain the additional savings needed in step 10.

_____ /yr.
_____ /mo.
_____ /wk.

do this even if you have a plan at work. Other than tax-deferred plans, we also need to consider our individual savings. Your Net Worth Statements will help you come up with the figure you have today in terms of investments that produce income. In addition, you need to evaluate any assets you'll be converting from a non-income-producing holding to an income-producing holding (such as real estate—you may sell a home, or rent out a vacation property).

Jane, are you ready to look at the Planning Your Retirement Worksheet?

JANE: As ready as I'll ever be. What do I do first?

ANN: Reader, you can follow along with Jane to see the process. Hers is opposite, yours is on p. 129.

STEP 1

The first thing we need to determine is your present annual income.

JANE: I make $35,000 at my job and approximately $7,500 in interest and dividends.

ANN: OK. Line 1 is $35,000 plus $7,500, or $42,500. Now, we're going to refer to the Future Value Table (p. 80). You will recall we used this table once before when we were learning how to finance one of our goals. Jane, do you get an increase in wages each year?

JANE: Usually a small amount. Last year it was only 3 percent.

ANN: All right. On the Future Value Table, refer to the column headed 3 percent. Since you already indicated that you would like to retire in three years, find the factor that intersects with three years and 3 percent growth. It is 1.0927. Multiply your present salary, $35,000, times 1.0927 and the result will be what you will be earning when you plan to retire in three years ($38,245). Now take your investment income. At what rate is this growing?

JANE: Only 5 percent. It's in a savings bank.

ANN: Look at the Future Value Table again. This time use the 5 percent column, and find the factor that corresponds to 5 percent and three years (1.1576). Multiply $7,500 times 1.1576 ($8,682). Add $8,682 and $38,245 to come up with what your total income would be in three years—$46,927. Put this on line 2.

Planning Your Retirement Worksheet JANE

1. Present annual gross income before taxes — $ *42,500*

2. Annual gross income prior to retirement (use Future Value Table, p. 80) — *46,927*

3. Annual retirement income needed (step 2 multiplied by 80%) — *37,542*

4. Assuming 5% inflation rate, the annual income you will need to retire (step 3 times multiplier in Future Value Table) — *43,459*

5. Estimated Social Security — *7,200*

6. Expected annual pension — *4,800*

7. Expected income from 401(k) or other employer plan — *6,000*

8. Estimated savings and investments expected at retirement that will provide income or be drawn from your principal — *290,000*

9. Estimated retirement income per year you can expect from your savings in step 8 — *23,200*

10. Add items in steps 5, 6, 7, and 9, and then subtract step 4. — *41,200 − 43,459 (2,259)*

11. If step 10 is a negative number (shortfall in the amount needed per year to retire), divide the shortfall by the percentage you estimate you could earn if this shortfall were invested. — *28,238*

12. Divide the result in step 11 by the appropriate annuity factor from the Annuity Factors Table (p. 82) table to determine how much you need to save each year from now to retirement to obtain the additional savings needed in step 10.

    2655 /yr.
    221 /mo.
    51 /wk.

STEP 2

To fill in line 3 you must ask yourself how much of the amount you currently earn you will need in retirement. Obviously, when you retire your needs will be different. Commuting costs will be eliminated, clothing costs will probably go down; however, health costs may increase,* and travel expenses usually go up. Many planners feel 60 percent of your present income is sufficient, but I don't think so. To be conservative, I think it is wise to use 80 percent of your income at retirement. On line 3, put 80 percent of $46,927 or $37,542.

STEP 3

We know that the prices of goods we buy go up every year. If everything costs more, but our income remains the same, obviously there will be a cash squeeze. In order to avoid this unhappy occurrence, we want to put in an inflation adjustment on the income we need in retirement.

Once again, turn to the Future Value Table. You can use any rate of inflation you choose (your guess is as good as that of any economist), but 5 percent is probably reasonable. So line 4 will be $37,542 multiplied by the factor corresponding to three years and 5 percent (1.1576). The result is that we want to aim to have an income of $43,459 when we retire in order to maintain the same lifestyle we now have. If you wish to live more expensively than you do now, this is the time to make that adjustment to the amount of income you will need. Analyze your present Cash Flow Worksheet and estimate where the changes will be. (This also applies if you contemplate scaling down your life-style.)

Jane, your income goal from all sources will be to have $43,459 per year. Fill that in on line 4. The next steps will determine if we have a surplus or deficit of funds.

STEP 4

Take the figure you obtained from your Social Security form for your benefit at age 65 and put it on line 5.

JANE: That would be $600 per month. So $600 multiplied by 12 months is $7,200.

ANN: Good. Line 6 is your annual pension amount. How much will you get?

---

* Be sure to have adequate health coverage when you retire. Even though you will have Medicare, you should also have *one* supplemental policy that will cover the items Medicare does not cover.

JANE: I won't know exactly until I retire, but it's estimated at around $400 per month, which would be $4,800 per year. I also have my 401(k). Does that go here also?

ANN: Put the amount of income that can be generated from your 401(k) on line 7. Because you are over $59\frac{1}{2}$, you'll be able to withdraw money without a penalty. For now, let's assume you will not touch any principal, but you will take the income (interest/dividends) generated, which has been around 8 percent. Your 401(k) balance is around $75,000. And 8 percent on $75,000 is $6,000, which goes on line 7.

Now, Jane, we want to look at your personal assets to see how much income can be generated.

JANE: Well, I have the life insurance my husband left me and a bit of other money. Together they amount to approximately $150,000. This is what I am currently earning 5 percent interest on at the bank. So the amount I am receiving is around $7,500.

ANN: I hope you gathered some information for diversifying into other investments that will also produce more income. Are there any sources other than this money?

JANE: I have an IRA that I did before the 401(k) was put into place at my firm. That has about $15,000 in it. I also rolled over my husband's retirement account into my own IRA, which is an additional $45,000, so the total is $60,000. When I sell the house, I will be replacing it with a much smaller one. Since I am over 55 years old, I believe I don't have to pay tax on the first $125,000 of gain on the sale. But I think the gain will be only about $80,000, since I still have the home improvement loan to pay off and values for houses in my area are not as high as they were. So, let's say I will add $80,000, to my assets for income.

ANN: Great. So, let's see where we stand: $150,000 plus $60,000 plus $80,000 equals $290,000. (Put that on line 8.) If you can earn 8 percent on your money, this would produce $23,200. Put this number on line 9.

STEP 5

Now, add all your income items:

Social Security (line 5)	$ 7,200
Pension (line 6)	4,800
401(k) (line 7)	6,000
Personal assets (line 9)	23,200
	$41,200
From this amount subtract the income needed (line 4):	(43,459)
	(2,259)

Fill in ($2,259) on line 10. All of your income sources add up to $41,200. However, if you continue your same life-style, you need $43,459 per year. Therefore, you have a shortfall of $2,259 per year.

As we have learned throughout this course, there are many ways to accomplish the goal of having income equal outgo. Any suggestions?

CAROL: Jane said she wanted to continue to work. She will have more than she needs if she works part-time.

TERRY: But if she decides not to work, she can spend a few thousand dollars less a year. I'm sure she could work that out of her budget.

SUSAN: Wait a minute. Is it so terrible to use some of the principal? Jane, do you want to leave money to your children, or do you feel comfortable using some of it?

JANE: Gee, I don't know. I don't want to run out of money. The way to assure that seemed to be *not* to touch principal. I would like to leave some money to my children, but that's not my number one concern.

ANN: These are all good suggestions. A word about dipping into principal: It's a definite alternative as long as you have planned how long you need the money to last. Look at the Earnings Rate Table on p. 135. Jane, in our original plan, you were using the income generated from all of your accounts, which we estimated at an 8 percent rate. If you continue to take out the 8 percent but leave the principal, obviously the money will never run out. But if instead you decide to use some of your principal, and based on life expectancy tables, you determine you will live for 28 years after retirement, you could withdraw 9 percent of your money per year (1 percent over your 8 percent earnings) and not run out. If you want the money to last for 20 years, you could withdraw 10 percent per year (2 percent over earnings).

While I agree with Jane that we want to protect our principal, I also agree with Susan that we want to enjoy our retirement, and using principal *with a plan in mind* is fine.

If, however, you would prefer not to touch the principal, you could continue to work and put more money into your investments to generate the additional $2,000 plus that you need. How much money would you need to invest to throw off the $2,259 shortfall if you could get income of 8 percent from your investment? Divide $2,259 by 8 percent ($2.259 ÷ .08 = $28,238). So, if you could come up with

EARNINGS RATE TABLE
How many years do you want your money to last?

Estimate how many years you need your money to last. Then, based on the interest rate you are earning on your retirement money, this table will tell you what percentage of the fund you can withdraw each year.

YEARS	EARNINGS RATE (%)							
	5	6	7	8	9	10	11	12
9	14	14.5	15	15	16	16.5	17	17.5
10	13	14	14	14.5	15.5	16	16.5	17
11	12	13	13	14	15	15	16	16.5
12	11	12	12	13	14.4	14.5	15	16
13	10.5	11	11.5	12.5	13.7	14	14.5	15.5
14	10	10.5	11	12	13	13.5	14	15
15	9.5	10	10.6	11.5	12.5	13	13.6	14.6
16	9	9.6	10.3	11	12	12.6	13.3	14.3
17	8.75	9.3	10	10.9	11.9	12.3	13	14
18	8.5	9	9.8	10.6	11.6	12	12.9	13.75
19	8.25	8.8	9.6	10.3	11.3	11.9	12.7	13.5
20	8	8.6	9.4	10	11	11.75	12.5	13.25
21	7.8	8.4	9.2	9.9	11	11.60	12.3	13
22	7.6	8.2	9	9.75	10.8	11.45	12.2	12.8
23	7.4	8	8.9	9.6	10.6	11.30	12	12.6
24	7.2	7.9	8.8	9.6	10.4	11.15	11.9	12.4
25	7	7.8	8.7	9.45	10.2	11	11.75	12.2
26	6.9	7.7	8.5	9.3	10	10.8	11.60	12
27	6.8	7.6	8.4	9.15	9.8	10.65	11.45	11.9
28	6.7	7.5	8.3	9	9.6	10.5	11.30	11.8
29	6.6	7.4	8.2	8.8	9.4	10.3	11.15	11.6
30	6.5	7.3	8	8.6	9.2	10.15	11	11.4

an additional $28,238 and put it with your other money earning 8 percent, you would balance your budget. (Put $28,238 on line 11.)

JANE: Could I do this by the time I am 70? I really would totally like to finish working by then.

ANN: Let's see. That's eight years from now. Turn to the Annuity Factors Table, p. 82. Check the intersection of eight periods and 8 percent and divide the factor (10.636) into the total amount of money you need—$28,238. ($28,238 ÷ 10.636 = $2,655.) This means that if you can add $2,655 per year to your retirement funds for the next eight years, you will reach your goal. (Put that amount on line 12 of your retirement worksheet). Divide $2,655 by 12 and that comes to $221 per month; divide $2,655 by 52 and that comes to $51 per week.

Jane, what do you think about the choices you have?

JANE: Well, I certainly am going to be working at least for the next three years. In that time, I can increase my contribution to my 401(k) plan as much as possible. That way, I will get my tax-deferred contribution, the match from my company, and the 8 percent investment return that I don't have to pay tax on until I begin to take my distribution. If I continue to work part-time until I'm 70, I'll be making more money than I need to live on, so I'll be able to invest the surplus for the future. I can probably put aside more than the $51 per week you calculated, and wind up with more than I need.

ANN: There's a lot to think about, and as you go forward, you may change how you feel about certain issues. The important part of this exercise is that you have a plan that can now be modified.

JANE: Also that I know the alternatives. Before, I was so confused about where to begin. It's hard to believe that I could be this organized about something I've worried about for so long.

ANN: Jane, you've done a great job. The rest of the group should follow your example and work on their own retirement planning. Don't wait until you're ready to retire, though. The sooner you begin, the easier it will be to accumulate the amount of money you will need. Jane had many resources, but she still needed to investigate others. Develop your resources early and make use of them to their fullest. You will be assuring yourself of a retirement worth looking forward to.

CAN A PROFESSIONAL
HELP YOU?

ANN: The number one question I hear from women all over the country is "If I need help, whom can I trust?"

TERRY: I understand why. People are always trying to sell you something, and they can be very convincing.

CAROL: Right. Then later you find out that you bought something that the salesperson made more on than you did.

ANN: I hear you. Obviously, this does happen often. All the more reason that *you* need to take responsibility for the investments you make. This doesn't mean that you cannot use professionals. I've said it before, and I'll say it again, I believe in employing people to help you. What I do *not* believe in is relinquishing the decisions to these people. *You* need to be the person in charge.

The first decision is finding the right person.

JANE: How do you go about that? I get two to three calls a week from people trying to sell me stocks or insurance.

ANN: I know. "Cold calling" is a marketing device used by many firms. Salespeople telephone lists of potential clients and pitch a product. Most people will not respond, but some will. As a general rule I would suggest that you not buy a product from someone over the phone. It's an invitation to disaster. If someone piques your interest, ask to have information about the firm and the recommendation sent to you. You'll be able to see the level of commitment by the broker and you'll give yourself time to think. If the salesperson tells you what a mistake you are making, that this is a once-in-a-lifetime opportunity, hang up as soon as possible—there is no such thing.

SUSAN: Then how *do* you find a competent person to help you?

ANN: The best away I know is to get a referral from someone you know who has had a good experience. Ask your friends, relatives, and other professionals (tax person, lawyer, etc.). Get at least three names and interview them in person, not over the phone.

CAROL: I find asking professionals questions intimidating. Sometimes I don't understand the answer and it's so mortifying that I can't think of anything else to say.

ANN: Look, the bottom line is that they want your business, and you need to communicate what it is you would like them to do. If you are not comfortable enough to accomplish that, you have not found the right person. Don't be intimidated. Move on. There are plenty of people who would love to work with you and will take the time to explain the alternatives they can offer. But *you* must take the responsibility to verbalize what you are trying to accomplish. That's another reason to have your goal list in shape and to be able to ask questions when you don't understand.

STACY: What if you don't have anyone to get referrals from?

ANN: Most of the professions have organizations that will give you the names of people in your area who are members in good standing of their group. You may need to interview many to find the right person, since the recommendation is not coming from someone you know.

I also encourage you to investigate continuing education classes in your area. Many topics can be taught in one or two sessions, and it's very helpful to have someone to whom you can ask questions.

Reader, thank you for joining our group, and give yourself a big pat on the back. These exercises have enabled you to set goals and establish a plan—one that will put *you* in control of your money.

FINANCIAL RESOURCES

—————■■■—————

This listing will provide you with assistance in finding someone to help you. I have put together a directory that is a guideline of the organizations for referral, the payment schedules, and the questions to ask when looking for a financial planner, insurance agent, tax preparer, lawyer, stockbroker, or investment advisor. Use it as a starting point. As you begin to investigate, you will add your own referral organizations, and, I hope, many more questions to ask. Phone numbers may change, but with persistence, you will be able to locate the organizations. (Try the 800 directory first: 800-555-1212.)

PROFESSION	ORGANIZATION FOR REFERRALS	HOW COMPENSATED	QUESTIONS TO ASK
Financial planner	American College (ChFC) 270 Bryn Mawr Ave. Bryn Mawr, PA 19010 215-526-1427 American Institute of Certified Public Accountants (APFS) 1211 Avenue of the Americas New York, NY 10019 800-522-5430 Institute of Certified Financial Planners (CFP) Two Denver Highlands 10065 East Harvard Ave., Ste. 320 Denver, CO 80231 800-282-7526 International Association for Financial Planning Two Concourse Parkway, Ste. 800 Atlanta, GA 30328 800-241-2148 National Association of Personal Financial Advisors (NAPFA) 1130 Lake Cook Rd., Ste. 105 Buffalo Grove, IL 60089 800-366-2732 To check on a particular planner, contact: Better Business Bureau, local telephone directory; or The Securities & Exchange Commission, 202-272-7450. Or check any of the above organizations to see if there are any complaints against planner.	1. Fee based rate/hour 2. Commission on products sold 3. Combination of fee and commission 4. Fee offset: commission offset planning charges 5. Salary: service of bank, credit union, etc.	1. Are you registered with the SEC? If no, why not? 2. What is your educational background? 3. What professional designations do you have? 4. What did you do before becoming a financial planner? 5. What is your professional experience? 6. What are your specialties? 7. How are you compensated? Are you fee based? Are you commission based? Are you fee and commission based? 8. If you are receiving commissions, do you disclose all compensation you receive from my account? 9. If you are fee based, do you provide referrals for other professionals? Will you interview these professionals with me? 10. How many sessions will we need to accomplish my goals? 11. How often will I see you after the initial plan is complete? 12. Can I call you with questions—how are you compensated for phone sessions? 13. May I have the names of 3 clients to call as referrals?

Profession	Organization for Referrals	How Compensated	Questions to Ask
Insurance agent	American College (CLU) 270 Bryn Mawr Ave. Bryn Mawr, PA 19010 215-526-1427 Department of Insurance (Your state) See telephone book. National Association of Life Underwriters 1922 F St., N.W. Washington, DC 20006 202-463-6100	1. Independent agent: Usually represents 2 or more insurance companies. Paid a commission on products sold. 2. Exclusive agent: Represents 1 company. (Offers product from that company first, but can represent other companies.) 3. Direct writer representative: Sells through own employees or mail. Salaried or commission. 4. Fee based: Charge for advice, no commission.	1. How much time and attention will you give me/my account? 2. Do you have a designation? (CLU: Chartered Life Underwriter CPCU: Certified Property/Casualty Underwriter ChFC: Chartered Financial Consultant CFP: Certified Financial Planner) 3. What is your specialty? Can you refer me to someone who can help me in another area? 4. What are the costs built into the product? 5. What is the financial rating of the insurer you are recommending? Check rating at library in: *A.M. Best* *Standard & Poor's* *Moody's* *Duff & Phelps* 6. If fee based, what is fee for initial interview, recommendation, and follow-up? 7. May I have the names of 3 clients to call as referrals?

Tax preparer	American Institute of Certified
	  Public Accountants (AICPA)
	1211 Avenue of the Americas
	New York, NY 10036
	800-862-4272
	
	National Association of Enrolled
	  Federal Tax Accountants
	6108 North Harding Ave.
	Chicago, IL 60659
	800-424-4339
	
	Local Chamber of Commerce
	See telephone book for listing.
	
	Tax Counseling for the Elderly
	Free services for seniors.
	Contact local IRS office.
		1. Fee based: rate per hour
		
		2. Rate per total job
		
		3. Rate per tax return (simple forms)
			1. What is your educational background?
			
			2. What is your professional background?
			
			3. What type of client do you specialize in (individual, small business, etc.)?
			
			4. Are you open year-round or only at tax time?
			
			5. How much do you charge? Hourly or flat fee?
			
			6. How many returns do you do a year?
			
			7. If I get audited, will you handle it and/or go with me? If so, what is the charge?

PROFESSION	ORGANIZATION FOR REFERRALS	HOW COMPENSATED	QUESTIONS TO ASK
Tax preparer (*cont.*)	VITA—Volunteer Income Tax Assistance Program For low-income, disabled, non-English-speaking people, contact local IRS office. For complaints: If CPA: state board of CPAs If not CPA: IRS State/city/county consumer affairs		8. How do you stay current on tax law changes? 9. May I have the names of 3 clients to call as referrals?
Lawyer	State/city/county Bar Association Lawyer referral and information service. For phone numbers, look in local telephone book or call National Bar Association, 312-988-5000. For specific type of lawyer (e.g., criminal, divorce, etc.), check encyclopedia of associations (at the library) for that group and ask for referrals. Local law school, dean's office. Ask for clinics. If you cannot afford a lawyer, contact the Legal Aid Society or Legal Services Corporation (federal program). For complaints: City, state or county Bar Association, or National Bar Association at: American Bar Association 750 North Lake Shore Dr. Chicago, IL 60611 312-988-5000	1. Hourly—can be from $50 to $300 per hr. Usually charge for each quarter hour plus disbursements. 2. Flat fee. 3. Contingency: lawyer collects a percentage of amount you are awarded (can be 25% to 50% of award). If you don't win, there is no charge, but you will have to pay court fees.	1. Do you charge for initial consultation? 2. What is your educational background? 3. What is your professional background? 4. Do you have a specialized area of expertise? How long have you practiced in this area? 5. If I have a problem outside of your expertise, can you refer me to a lawyer who can handle my case? 6. Will you handle my case personally, or will other lawyers/paralegals be working on it? 7. How much do you charge (flat fee, hourly, contingency)? What is fee for work done by an associate/a paralegal? Request a letter of retention specifically stating amounts charged for each professional. Request a monthly itemized bill. (It is advisable to pay by check or get a receipt for payment.) 8. How long will it take to complete my case? How much do you estimate it will cost? Can I have the estimate, including expenses, in writing? Can we set a maximum amount to be charged? 9. May I have the names of 3 clients to call as referrals?

Profession	Organization for Referrals	How Compensated	Questions to Ask
Stockbroker	No organization. Once you have found broker from referral of a financial planner, lawyer, accountant, or personal friends, you can check on broker by contacting: North American Securities Administrators Association 202-737-0900 National Association of Securities Dealers 800-289-9999	1 to 3% on listed stocks Up to 5% on over-the-counter stocks Up to 8.5% on mutual funds Full service: Gives recommendations, information. Most will discount commissions if you ask. Discount brokerage: Only buys and sells securities. No information. Can be 50 to 60% off full commissions.	1. What is your educational background? What did you do before becoming a broker? How long have you been a broker? 2. What commissions do you charge? How much of a discount on commissions can I get? Are there any other fees I will have to pay for this account (custodial fees)? 3. Have you had any disciplinary action taken against you by any regulatory organization? 4. How many clients do you have? To whom do I speak if you are not available? How often will you meet with me? 5. Do you specialize in a certain type of account (stocks: growth, income, etc.; bonds: govt., corp., municipal, etc.)? Do you specialize in investing for retirement, college planning, income, speculation? What is the average size account you handle? 6. Where do you get your investment ideas? Does your firm have a research department? What percentage of investment ideas are from your own firm? Is there an approved list of stocks? 7. Will you call me before any purchases or sales are made for my account? Do you buy and hold stocks or trade frequently? 8. May I see 3 typical client's portfolios? How has the performance been? 9. If I transfer my account, can all the securities you purchase for me be transferred? 10. May I have the names of 3 clients to call as referrals?

PROFESSION	ORGANIZATION FOR REFERRALS	HOW COMPENSATED	QUESTIONS TO ASK
Investment advisor	Investment Counsel Association of America 20 Exchange Pl. New York, NY 10005 212-344-0999 *Directory of Registered Investment Advisors* (Standards of measurement and use for investment performance data.) Available at library. CDA Investment Technologies, Inc. 11501 Georgia Ave. Silver Springs, MD 20902 301-942-1700 (Records of money managers. Ranks top 20 managers for 1, 3, 5 years. Cost: $195.)	For most advisors, you need to invest at least $500,000; many have $1 million minimum. Fee: 1 to 2% plus commissions. Wrap accounts (mgmt. and transaction costs): 3%	1. Are you a registered investment advisor? 2. How long have you been in business? 3. What is the minimum size account? 4. What is your management fee? 5. How much insurance does each account have? 6. What firm serves as custodian of the securities? 7. How much are the custodial fees? 8. How much are commissions on transactions? 9. What types of securities do you buy? Where do you get your investment ideas? 10. Do all your clients have the same portfolio or are they different for each client? 11. Do you try to time the market? 12. How long do you typically hold your selections? 13. May I see a typical portfolio? 14. What has been the annual average return for 1, 3, 5, and 10 years vs. S&P 500 index? 15. How has performance been in down markets? 16. Is there any current litigation against you or your firm? 17. May I have the names of 3 clients to call as referrals?

FINANCIAL AND RELATED ORGANIZATIONS

––––––––

Here is a list of resources to obtain further information. These resources will help you to get more facts about a particular subject or can be used as a reference guide.

RESOURCES

Credit

Federal Trade Commission
Bureau of Consumer Protection
Division of Credit Practices
Pennsylvania Ave. at Sixth St., N.W.
Washington, DC 20580
202-523-3747

Handles complaints re Truth-in-Lending Laws.

Consumer Credit Handbook
Item # 441Y504
Consumer Information Center
Pueblo, CO 81002

Tells how to fix errors on credit report and how to proceed if turned down for credit card.

Consumer Credit Counseling Service
800-388-2227

Directs you to the nearest local office.

The Bank Rate Monitor
Box 088888
North Palm Beach, FL 33408

For $4, will send you a list of institutions that offer secured credit cards.

Card Track
Box 1700
Frederick, MD 21702

Tracks bank card interest rates nationwide; $5 per issue.

Bankcard Holders of America
560 Herndon Pkwy., Ste. 120
Herndon, VA 22070

For $4.50, will send you a brochure on how to get a low-interest-rate card.

CREDIT REPORTS
The following credit services will provide you with a credit report. If you have been denied credit, the credit report is supplied free. If you have not recently been denied credit, the credit bureau charges the fee cited.

TRW
800-422-4879
Free (no more than one a year)

Trans Union
312-431-5100
$15 single, $20 married

Equifax
800-685-1111
$3–$8, depending on where you live

CSC Credit Service
800-231-6783
$8 single, $16 married

Insurance

Insurance Information Institute
110 William St.
New York, NY 10038
800-331-9146

Provides brochures on different types of insurance.

National Insurance Consumer Organization
121 North Payne St.
Alexandria, VA 22314
703-549-8050

Provides brochures and information. Will analyze cash value of life insurance policies ($35 for first policy, $25 for each additional one).

Quotesmith
800-556-9393

Charges $15 for quotes on policies sold by independent agents.

Your state insurance commissioner's office
Handles inquiries regarding insurance companies.

Legal

American Arbitration Association
140 W. 51st St.
New York, NY 10020
212-484-4000

Arbitrates civil disputes

American Bar Association
Standing Committee on Dispute Resolution
1800 M St., N.W.
Washington, DC 20036
202-331-2258

Lists dispute-resolution centers throughout the country.

American Bar Association
American Bar Center
750 North Lake Shore Dr.
Chicago, IL 60611
312-988-5000

Provides information on how to choose a lawyer.

Martindale-Hubbell Directory
Available at library

Provides ratings on lawyers.

Retirement

American Association of Retired Persons
Fulfillment Department
1909 K St., N.W.
Washington, DC 20049
202-434-3525

Publishes a catalogue of publications, or provides individual publications, such as: *The Social Security Book: What Every Woman Absolutely Needs to Know* (# D 14117); *Focus Your Future: A Woman's Guide to Retirement Planning* (# D 14559); and *A Woman's Guide to Pension Rights* (# D 12258).

National Council on the Aging
600 Maryland Ave., S.W.
Washington, DC 20024
202-479-1200

Provides pamphlets on various topics

Investments

MUTUAL FUNDS

Morningstar Mutual Funds Rating Service
Library or $395 per year
800-876-5005

CDA Wiesenberger Mutual Funds
Library or $295 per year
800-232-2285

Standard & Poor's/Lipper Mutual Fund Profiles
Library or $132 per year
800-221-5277

The Handbook for No-Load Fund Investors
No-Load Fund Investor
P.O. Box 318
Irvington, NY 10533
$49

The Individual Investor's Guide to No-Load Mutual Funds
American Association of Individual Investors
612 N. Michigan Ave.
Chicago, IL 60611
$24.95

See also the book by Carole Gould in the list on the next page.

STOCKS

Value Line
Library or $495 per year (10-week trial for $60)
800-825-8354

Standard & Poor's Stock Guide
Library or $99 per year
800-221-5277

Schwab's Investment Research Reports Service
$5.50 per report on individual company
800-442-5111

Standard & Poor's Research Reports
$10 per report on individual company
800-642-2858

Brokerage firm investment material.

See also the books by Benjamin Graham and Peter Lynch in the list on the next page.

Investment Clubs

American Association of Individual Investors
612 N. Michigan Ave.
Chicago, IL 60611
312-280-0170

National Association of Investment Clubs
P.O. Box 220
Royal Oak, MI 48068
313-543-0612

Reference Books

(These may also be available at your local library.)

Gould, Carole. *The New York Time's Guide to Mutual Funds.* New York: Times Books/Random House, 1992.
Graham, Benjamin. *The Intelligent Investor.* New York: Harper & Row, 1973.
Lynch, Peter. *One Up on Wall Street.* New York: Simon & Schuster, 1989.
Pond, Jonathan D. *The New Century Family Money Book.* New York: Dell, 1993.
Ortaldo, Robert, Jr., CPA. *How to Live Within Your Means and Still Finance Your Dreams.* New York: Fireside, 1990.
Quinn, Jane Bryant. *Making the Most of Your Money.* New York: Simon & Schuster, 1991.
Savage, Terry. *Terry Savage Talks Money.* New York: HarperPerennial, 1991.

Computer Programs

Quicken
Checkbook management/financial analysis
List $69.95

Managing Your Money
Financial planning
List $79.95

Computer Associates—Simply Money
(Windows only)
Financial planning
List $49

Kiplinger Tax Cut
Tax returns
$39.95
800-365-1546

TurboTax
Tax returns
$49.95
800-964-1040

GLOSSARY

———————

ADJUSTED GROSS INCOME: Income after subtracting all adjustments, such as IRA or Keogh contributions, alimony payments, or business expenses.

ADR (American depository receipts): Shares of non-U.S. companies, dollar denominated for dividends and trading, that facilitate U.S. ownership of foreign companies because they trade on U.S. exchanges.

AFTER-TAX YIELD: The amount earned relative to what was invested, expressed as a percentage, and with taxes deducted from the result. For example, $100 earned on a $1,000 investment is a 10% return; after-tax (if tax is 28%) would be $100 – $28, or $72, for a 7.2% return.

ANNUAL PERCENTAGE RATE: What it costs per year for credit if you don't pay off the balance each month.

ANNUITY: Investment in which policyholder (annuitant) makes a lump-sum payment or installment payments to an insurance company and receives income at retirement for a certain period of time or for life. Fixed annuities are invested conservatively and guarantee payments, which consist of your principal investment plus interest. Variable annuities are invested in more aggressive investments and have no guaranteed payments. The portfolio grows free of taxes until the money is withdrawn.

ASSET: Anything you own that has a monetary value. A current asset can be turned into cash easily.

ASSET ALLOCATION: The mix of diversified investments in a financial portfolio.

ASSET MANAGEMENT ACCOUNT: An account offered at some brokerages, banks, and mutual funds that includes a checking account, a money-market account, and a brokerage account. Funds can move among accounts.

BACK-END LOAD: A charge imposed by a mutual fund when the shares are sold.

BALANCED FUND: A type of mutual fund that invests for growth and income. Investments usually include common stocks, preferred stocks, and bonds.

BALANCE SHEET: A financial statement that lists assets (what is owned), liabilities (what is owed), and net worth (assets minus liabilities). Also called net worth statement.

BEAR MARKET: A market where stock prices are declining for a time period of months or longer.

BENEFICIARY: The person who receives an inheritance or proceeds from a trust or an insurance policy.

BLUE CHIP: The common stock of a highly regarded company that has a history of dependable earnings and stable dividends.

BOND: A debt of a corporation or government. The purchaser lends money to the institution and it agrees to pay interest at specified intervals and to repay the principal amount at maturity.

BOND FUND: A type of mutual fund that invests in bonds. Its mission is creating income and preserving capital.

BROKER: An agent who buys and sells investment products for a commission.

BULL MARKET: A market where stock prices are rising for a time period of months or longer.

CALLABLE BOND: A bond that may be redeemed before maturity date by the issuer. Most bonds have call dates to protect the issuer from paying high interest rates for an extended period of time when rates are falling.

CAPITAL GAIN (LOSS): The profit or loss from the sale of a capital asset.

CERTIFICATE OF DEPOSIT: A bank deposit for a fixed period of time with a guaranteed interest rate. There is a penalty for early withdrawal.

COLLATERAL: An asset used to secure a loan. If payment is not made, the asset can be seized.

COLLATERALIZED MORTGAGE OBLIGATION (CMO): A security that is based on a pool of mortgages divided into short-term, medium-term, and long-term maturities. The investor receives interest and a portion of the principal with each payment, but each group differs as to when the principal is repaid.

COMMON STOCK: Equity interest in a corporation. Investors may receive dividends, vote on major issues facing the company and share in the growth of the company.

COMPOUND INTEREST: The computation of interest applied to the principal and the previously earned interest. The more frequently money is compounded, the more interest will be earned.

CONVERTIBLE BOND: A debt of the corporation that pays a lower interest rate than normal for the promise to "convert" the bond to a stock (equity ownership) if the stock price rises to a certain level.

COUPON RATE: The interest paid annually on a bond; expressed in a percentage.

CUSTODIAL ACCOUNT: An account in the name of a child that is held by a parent or trustee as custodian. Taxes on income and gains are paid by the child, who is usually in a lower tax bracket than the parent.

CYCLICAL STOCKS: The stock of companies whose earnings fluctuate sharply with the economy (e.g., housing, autos, capital equipment).

DEFERRED BILLING: Billing that occurs in a future month.

DEFERRED PAYMENT: Allows skipping a payment; interest continues to accrue.

DISCOUNT RATE: The interest rate charged by the Federal Reserve to depository institutions (banks, S&Ls, etc.). It acts as a floor for the rates these institutions charge their customers.

DIVERSIFICATION: Investing in varied types of instruments in order to spread the risk. This includes stocks, bonds, mutual funds, etc.

DIVIDEND: A distribution by a corporation of a portion of their earnings. May be in the form of cash or additional stock.

DOLLAR COST AVERAGING: Buying securities at scheduled intervals using the same dollar amount each time. The effect is to buy more shares when the prices are low and fewer when the prices are high.

DOW JONES AVERAGE: The average of thirty stocks that are chosen as representative of the major blue-chip companies in the U.S. Tracks the changes in value in the stock market.

EARNINGS PER SHARE: The net income of a company (after taxes are paid and preferred dividends are distributed) divided by the total number of shares outstanding in the company.

EASY MONEY: When the Federal Reserve allows sufficient funds to build in the banking system. Has the effect of lowering interest rates and making loans easier to obtain.

EMPLOYEE STOCK OWNERSHIP PLAN (ESOP): A program for employees to purchase stock in their own company through payroll deductions.

EQUITY: The ownership of common stock or preferred stock in a company. In real estate, the value of a property less any claims against it.

EX-DIVIDEND: "Without dividend," meaning stock is trading at a price that reflects that the buyer will not receive the dividend for the current quarter because of the time necessary to process the change in ownership of the shares.

EXECUTOR: In a will, the person named to administer the estate according to written instructions.

FACE VALUE: The value of a bond, stock, or insurance policy, which appears on the "face" of the certificate. This is different from the market value, which reflects the valuation based on current market conditions.

FAMILY OF FUNDS: Mutual funds owned by the same investment company. Each fund has a different objective, and investors can move their money from one to another by telephone instruction.

FEDERAL RESERVE: The money center of the United States where the currency is issued, U.S. government securities are sold (Treasury bills, Treasury notes, and Treasury bonds), and monetary policy is made and administered.

401(K):   A benefit plan in a company where the employee can make contributions on a tax-deferred basis from her paycheck and allow them to accumulate on a tax-free basis until they are withdrawn. In many cases, the company will match a percentage of the employee's contributions.

FRONT-END LOAD: A sales charge imposed by a mutual fund, an annuity, a life insurance policy, or a limited partnership upon purchase.

GOVERNMENT BOND: A bond sold by the U.S. government. Can be a Savings bond, a Treasury bill, a Treasury note, or a Treasury bond.

GRACE PERIOD: Time before interest begins to be charged. Usually 25 to 30 days.

GRANTOR: In a trust, the person who creates and endows the conditions.

GROWTH STOCK: A company whose earnings are growing at a fast pace and whose mission is to continue to plow back its earnings into the company to expand. It usually pays no dividend but has the potential for significant capital gains long-term.

GUARANTEED INVESTMENT CONTRACTS (GIC):   Contracts issued and guaranteed by insurance companies with maturities from 1 to 7 years.

ILLIQUID: An investment that cannot be easily converted into cash without the possibility of a significant loss of principal.

INCOME FUND: A type of mutual fund that invests to maximize income payment (dividends and interest) and keeps risk at a minimum.

INDEX FUND: A type of mutual fund that tries to mirror the performance of a particular stock index (e.g., Dow Jones or S&P 500) by holding the same percentage position of individual stocks as that index.

INDIVIDUAL RETIREMENT ACCOUNT (IRA):   A tax-deferred pension account that allows an individual to invest up to $2,000 per year ($2,250 if the spouse is not employed) in an account and not pay tax on the accumulation until withdrawal at retirement. There are severe penalties for withdrawal before age $59\frac{1}{2}$. Distributions must begin by age $70\frac{1}{2}$. The contribution is an adjustment to earned income (get deduction for tax purposes) *only* if you do not have another pension/401(k)/Keogh, etc., plan that is currently getting contributions. In addition, if you do not have a plan but your spouse does, you *cannot* take the deduction. If you participate in a company plan but you earn less than $25,000 (single) or $40,000 (married), you can deduct your contribution. There are partial deductions, which phase out at incomes of $35,000 (single) and $50,000 (married).

INFLATION: When the prices for goods and services rise throughout the economy.

INTESTACY: Dying without a will. The estate is distributed according to the laws of the state.

INVESTMENT CLUB: Individuals who pool their money and consistently add to it to make investments that are researched by members and then voted on by the group.

JOINT TENANCY: Co-ownership of property where each person owns an equal share of the whole property. Upon death, the survivors become owners of the deceased's share. It is not bequeathed to others, nor is it subject to probate.

JUNK BOND: A bond issued by a corporation that has a high risk of default. These bonds are rated BB, Ba, or lower and pay a much higher percentage of interest than bonds of higher quality.

KEOGH PLAN: A tax-deferred retirement plan for the self-employed. It allows much larger contributions than an IRA.

LIQUID ASSET: An investment that is cash or can be converted into cash easily without losing its value—for example, money-market, Treasury bill, short-term CD.

LISTED STOCK: A security that is traded on an organized exchange, such as the New York Stock Exchange or the American Stock Exchange.

LIVING TRUST: A trust established by the grantor during her lifetime that distributes the estate at her death without going through probate. All assets owned must be registered in the name of the trust, and a will is still necessary for any items that are not covered by the trust.

LOAD: In a mutual fund, the commission charged to pay for sales costs. A fund that charges no commission up front to purchase is called no-load. It may, however, have other charges, such as redemption fees, or 12(b)1 fees. All funds, whether load or no-load, charge annual management fees.

MANAGEMENT FEE: In a mutual fund, the annual charge to manage the fund. Usually ranges from 0.5 to 1.5 percent per year.

MATURITY: Regarding a loan or a bond, the date on which it must be paid in full by the borrower.

MONEY-MARKET DEPOSIT ACCOUNT: A savings account offered by a bank (federally insured) that usually pays higher interest than a regular savings account.

MONEY-MARKET FUND: A type of mutual fund that invests in various short-term securities that are highly liquid and provide better yields and more diversification for the individual investor.

MORTGAGE: A long-term loan made for a property that uses the property as collateral.

MUNICIPAL BOND: A bond issued by a state or local government that pays interest that is exempt from federal tax and usually from state and local tax. If you purchase a municipal bond where you live, you will normally receive the triple-tax exemption. Sold in denominations of $1,000 and $5,000.

MUTUAL FUND: An organization that invests the funds of many individuals into stocks, bonds, or other securities. The advantages are diversification, professional management, and usually reasonable fees.

NASDAQ (National Association of Securities Dealers Automated Quotations): A computerized system that provides quotes for securities in the over-the-counter (OTC) market. Since these stocks are not traded on an organized exchange, traders call up via computer the information needed to buy and sell securities.

NET ASSET VALUE: The value of a mutual fund's portfolio, determined by pricing all the securities, subtracting any liabilities, and dividing the amount by the number of shares outstanding.

NET INCOME: A company's income less its costs and expenses.

NET WORTH: Assets minus liabilities.

NEW ISSUE: A stock or bond sold to the public by a corporation for the first time.

NO-LOAD: A mutual fund that does not charge a sales fee upon purchase.

ODD LOT: Purchase of securities in an amount other than the standard trading unit of 100 shares.

OPTION: A contract giving the right to buy or sell a security or property at a specified price within a specified time.

OVER-THE-COUNTER: A market for securities that are not traded on a formal exchange. The shares are traded between dealers using computers and telephones.

PAPER PROFIT: The unrealized gain on a security that becomes realized only when sold.

PAR: The dollar amount printed on the face of a stock or bond certificate. For bonds, it also represents the redemption value at maturity.

PENNY STOCK: A highly speculative security that sells for under $1 per share.

PENSION: Regular payments made to a retired employee by her former employer.

POINTS: A charge by the mortgage lender to the buyer. One point is equal to 1 percent of the amount of the loan.

PORTFOLIO: All of the investment holdings of an individual or institution.

PREFERRED STOCK: A security in a company representing equity ownership with a claim on the company's earnings before payment can be made to common stockholders. In case of liquidation of the company, preferred shareholders are paid before common shareholders. Usually pays a fixed dividend, but holders cannot vote on stockholder issues.

PRICE-EARNINGS RATIO: The current market price divided by the earnings per share. Used as a measurement of how expensive a stock is. The higher the number, the more one pays. For example, if a company earns $1 per share and sells for $10 per share, one pays 10 times earnings. If the same company sold for $20, one would pay 20 times earnings.

PRIME RATE: The interest rate charged by banks to their most creditworthy customers.

PRINCIPAL: Capital that is lent or invested. The principal amount of an investment would be the par value.

PROSPECTUS: An offering document that includes facts about the company or fund under consideration.

PROXY: A document authorizing the vote of a shareholder at a stockholders' meeting.

RATING: Assessment by independent companies (Moody's and Standard & Poor are the two largest) of the financial strength of a bond. Moody's ratings range from Aaaa to C, and S&P's from AAA to D.

REAL RATE OF RETURN: The return on an investment adjusted for inflation.

RECESSION: A far-reaching decline in economic activity, when unemployment rises and product output falls.

RECORD DATE: The date on which a shareholder must be registered on the company's books in order to receive dividends or vote.

REDEMPTION: The repurchase by the issuer of a bond.

REGISTERED BOND: A bond that is recorded on the books of the issuer in the owner's name. All interest payments are made directly to the owner, and upon sale the owner must endorse the bond.

REIT (real estate investment trust):   A REIT invests in and manages real estate and mortgages.

ROLLOVER: Refunding of an investment at maturity into the same investment with a new maturity (e.g., Treasury bills, CDs).

ROLLOVER IRA: Moving the assets from one qualified retirement plan to another. Having your ex-employer make the transfer within 60 days avoids any tax consequences.

ROUND LOT: In stock trading, 100 shares of stock or multiples of 100; in bonds, 1,000 par value or multiples of 1,000.

RULE OF 72:   Used to determine how many years it takes for money to double at a particular interest rate. Divide 72 by the interest rate you can earn—e.g., divide 72 by 8 percent interest and the result is that it will take nine years to double your money. To determine how long to make your money triple, divide 115 by the appropriate interest rate.

SAVINGS BOND: A U.S. government security. EE bonds are purchased at a discount from face value. If they are held for five years, they earn interest based on 85 percent of the five-year Treasury bond rate, but not less than 6 percent. HH bonds are purchased at par value and interest is paid every six months.

SEC (Securities and Exchange Commission): The U.S. federal regulatory agency responsible for regulation and enforcement of laws pertaining to the securities industry.

SEP (Simplified Employee Pension Plan): A retirement plan for the self-employed where an IRA is established for each employee and a percentage of earnings is contributed up to a maximum amount.

SHAREHOLDER: The owner of equity (shares or units) in a corporation or a mutual fund.

SPLIT: Dividing the company's shares into a larger number of shares without changing the overall ownership in the corporation. The purpose is to lower the stock price and attract new investors.

STOCK: An ownership interest in a corporation. Upon purchase, one participates in the share appreciation when earnings increase and the news is positive, or the share depreciation when earnings decrease and the news is negative.

STOCK CERTIFICATE: The piece of paper showing ownership in a corporation.

STREET NAME: Securities held in the broker's name instead of the customer's name, usually to facilitate selling.

SURRENDER VALUE: The cash value in an insurance policy that the owner would receive if the policy were redeemed prior to death.

TAX-DEFERRED: Payment of taxes not due until a time in the future.

TAX-EXEMPT: Not subject to payment of income taxes.

TERM INSURANCE: Pure life insurance with no accumulation of cash value. The benefit is paid only upon the death of the insured person.

TESTAMENTARY TRUST: A trust that becomes effective upon the death of the grantor.

TIGHT MONEY: When the Federal Reserve restricts the money supply. The result makes less money available in the system and it is more difficult to get a loan.

TOTAL RETURN: Entire amount earned on an investment—that is, the sum of the capital gain (or loss), the dividends, and the interest.

TREASURY BILL: A short-term debt instrument issued by the U.S. government that has maturities of three months, six months, or one year. The minimum purchase is $10,000; they are sold at a discount to face value (difference between face value and amount of interest to be earned over the period). When they are redeemed, you receive the full face value.

TREASURY BOND: A long-term debt instrument issued by the U.S. government with maturities of 10 to 30 years. They are sold in denominations of $1,000, pay interest twice annually, and are traded in the secondary market, with price fluctuations based on the rise or fall of interest rates.

TREASURY NOTE: A medium-term debt instrument issued by the U.S. government with maturities of 1 to 10 years. The minimum purchase for notes with a maturity under four years is $5,000; for notes with a maturity over four years, it is $1,000. Interest is paid twice annually, and they trade in the secondary market like Treasury bonds.

TRUST: A legal transfer of property from the person establishing the trust (grantor) to the person responsible for investment and administration (trustee) for the benefit of a third person (beneficiary).

UNEARNED INCOME: Income received that is not compensation for production of goods or services. For example, interest or dividends on investments is unearned income, whereas wages from work would be earned income. Also called passive income.

UNIFORM GIFTS TO MINORS ACT: A law in many states that outlines the rules on how to transfer assets to minor children.

UNIT TRUST: An investment in a share of a fixed portfolio (usually bonds) that pays a specific rate of interest over a specific time period. As individual bonds mature, there are partial redemptions, and the trust dissolves when all the bonds mature.

UNIVERSAL LIFE INSURANCE: A life insurance policy where part of the premium goes to purchase the insurance and the rest is put into an investment program.

VOLUME: The number of shares traded in a security over a period of time.

WARRANT: A certificate representing the right to buy securities at a specified price (exercise price) within a certain time period. It is sometimes offered with other securities to make it more attractive and may trade separately.

WHOLE LIFE INSURANCE: A life insurance policy where the premiums continue at the same level throughout the life of the holder.

WILL: A legal document that specifies the distribution of assets upon death.

YIELD: The amount earned (expressed as a percentage) as interest (bond) or dividend (stock). To calculate, take the amount of interest/dividend earned and divide by the current price.

YIELD TO MATURITY: The rate of return on a long-term investment that takes into account the purchase price, the interest payments, the redemption price, and the amount of time until redemption.

ZERO COUPON BOND: A bond (corporate, municipal, or Treasury) sold at a deep discount from face value that pays out no interest until maturity, when it is redeemed at full face value. Taxes must be paid, however, on the amount of interest that accrues to the bond each year (only taxable bonds).

INDEX

——— —— ——

ABOUT THE AUTHOR

———

Before becoming a financial counselor, Ann B. Diamond was a portfolio manager, vice president, and director of a private investment-banking firm. She worked in the institutional brokerage and private banking fields for more than fifteen years.

Ann currently manages her own business as a chartered financial consultant. In addition to counseling private clients, she conducts workshops in financial management at private and nonprofit organizations, professional associations, and schools. She travels nationwide presenting a seminar titled "Money Matters for Women" sponsored by Citibank MasterCard and Visa. She has also taught courses at the New School in New York City.

Ann has appeared on numerous radio and television programs across the country, including CNN, "9 Broadcast Plaza," "Money Talks," and "The Nightly Business Report." She is a member of the International Association for Financial Planning, the American Society of CLU & ChFC, NAFE, and the Financial Women's Association of New York. She lives with her husband in New York City.